So Far So Good

SO FAR

Recollections of a Life

Westport, Connecticut

SO GOOD

in Publishing by Edwin Seaver

with a preface by Angus Cameron

Lawrence Hill & Company

Published by
Lawrence Hill & Company, Inc.
520 Riverside Avenue, Westport, CT 06880

Library of Congress Cataloging-in-Publication Data

Seaver, Edwin.
  So far, so good.

  1. Seaver, Edwin—Biography. 2. Authors, American—
20th century—Biography. 3. Publishers and publishing—
United States—Biography. I. Title.
PS3537.E17S6 1986   818'.5209   [B]   86-12068
ISBN 0-88208-207-8

Printed in the United States of America

Preface by Angus Cameron

Edwin Seaver could have written a typical publishing memoir, filled with inside stories about celebrities outside the ken of most people, but he elected not to do this. True, there is much of the literary life in this unusual autobiography, but, as interesting as this aspect of the memoir is, it is incidental in a sense. Mr. Seaver's intention here is to half-heed Socrates when the philosopher said that the unexamined life is not worth living. Reserving judgement about his own examination, the author says that for him "one could just as well say the *examined* life was not worth living, it is so 'sicklied o'er with the pale cast of thought' as to 'lose the name of action.'" "But assuming," writes Mr. Seaver, "for the moment that examination is all, if only it could come before, when presumably it might affect our acts, instead of after the die is cast. Perhaps it can for a Socrates. But for most of us the act has first to be lived, life has to have happened to us, before it can be examined and its 'worth' weighed.

"I argue against my better judgement that if I can see where I erred in the past (or where, presiding in the court of the present, judge I went wrong), I can avoid making the same mistake in the future.

PREFACE

"When any man tells me he was a fool yesterday, he wants me to know that today he is wise. This is a dubious assumption on his part, as questionable as the notion that we learn from experience. Examining my own life, I see the anguish arises less from the recognition that I have behaved like an idiot than from the intimation that I shall go on being the same kind of idiot all my days."

The way Edwin Seaver remembers his life is very satisfactory to the reader of his gentle, and satiric memoir, for it excuses our own lapses about our own lives. Mr. Seaver (Ed from here on, for he is an old friend of mine) has his cake while he eats it: he provides us with a chronology but he does not permit the passage of time to enslave him.

He has a talent for remembering how he was and how he felt at different times in his life. While he gives us a beginning, middle, and end in his book, and the end is not yet, for Ed seems to wear his 86 years lightly, he does not allow the chronology of events to seem too important.

His memoir reads as if he had not used diaries, old letters, notes, and newspaper clippings to remind him of the events he lived through; rather he offers us what he wants to remember, and what he wants to remember about himself is entertaining although what he leaves out about his professional career may sometimes seem arbitrary. But since there is little about his life that he has controlled, he may be forgiven for controlling what he chooses to remember.

I remember him when we were colleagues at Little, Brown & Co. in Boston as the only well-informed literary man (including myself, I might add) on the entire staff. While as head of advertising and promotion,—the position he held and that I had a hand in his getting ("At 50," he said, "I just have this job for at my age it is undoubtedly the last good position that will be offered to me.") Ed combined with his literary sensibilities excellent additional qualities. He had the right amount of larceny in his blood to write good copy and recognize good copy when someone else wrote it. Like any good advertising and promotion man, Ed had a con man's psyche.

There is a neatness to the author's outlook. It is easy to think of him as cynical, for he seems at times to be throwing away seriousness of any kind, but it is not true   Ed is rather a man who knows that both optimism and pessimism are equally premature. He wouldn't be surprised at all if he concluded that life, after all, had been worth living, but he'd never bet on it.

In his introduction, after telling a tale about not recognizing the man he saw approaching him across a hotel lobby as a reflection of himself in a ceiling-high mirror, he did find that mirror image familiar. And this may be extended as a metaphor; he is familiar with himself all through this memoir even though he is never sure who he is.

"Know Thyself," counselled the Delphic oracle.

"Know myself indeed!" says Ed. "I who am such a bundle of contradictions, such a medley of selves each claiming to be the authentic I, the genuine Who!

Which self is sovereign when all are pretenders?"

The reader may say, "Well, any memoir writer who can say that all his medley of selves are pretenders must be an honest man." This reaction wouldn't mean too much to the author of this memoir, for he is genuinely more interested in being honest with himself than he is with the good opinion of his readers. He seems to be addressing an exterior audience, his reader, and interior one, himself. Which self he never quite says, but the reader will be pleased with it, I am sure.

Ed Seaver became conscious of literature and politics in World War One and thus far has survived two World Wars, the Great Depression, two police actions, and the threat of World War III. His life has been an interlarding of literature with politics, although in no sense is he a 'political'. Freelance magazine writer, novelist, editor, teacher, critic, publicity man, his jobs have ranged from the old *Socialist Call* and, later, the *Leader,* to *Soviet Russia Today* and the *Daily Worker* to a job with the Book-of-the-Month Club, and, later, with a major U.S. book publisher. The author makes it clear that he did not leave his job with the *Daily Worker* for ideological reasons but rather because the Book-of-the-Month Club offered more money. Ed has always been in the last analysis 'of the Left' and has twice been penalized for his convictions. He is, however, a survivor.

For older readers sensitive to the issues of our times in both literature and politics, his memoir will be a vivid reminder of times past. I think that his book will also appeal to those of the current generation who have the wit to know that love did not begin when they had their first sexual experience and that politics did not begin with the 1984 election.

I began to write at a moment when my own story seemed to have come to an end . . . But when experience ends, the understanding of what we have experienced and done has scarcely begun: that penultimate judgment in which we are ourselves judge and accused and sole witness.

KATHLEEN RAINE

Every morning first thing I do on rising is look for my face in the bathroom mirror. To see if I'm still there? God knows how long I've been cutting this caper. I became aware of it only today when I caught myself in the act.

As I scanned the image in the glass I thought if I should chance to see that face in a crowd would I recognize it as mine? No more, probably, than if I were to hear a babel of voices on a recording I could readily identify one of them as my own.

Like the time I encountered the stranger in the hotel corridor.

My guest at lunch was a "business contact," and I was resigned to the prospect of yet another expense account meal which begins with too much to drink, continues with too much to eat, and ends with too much boredom. After which, as a colleague complained, all you can do is toss and turn at your desk the rest of the afternoon.

As we came into the thickly carpeted, rather spacious and well-lighted passage between the hotel lobby and the restaurant favored by my guest I caught sight of a man coming toward us who looked vaguely familiar. From his tentative smile I gathered

I

he recognized me, or thought he did. While I, in turn, felt certain we had met before, though I could not recall where, or when, or in what connection, or even what his name was. Perplexed that I was so totally unable to place him it was with some perturbation I watched him draw near as if to greet me.

Not only could I not remember his name, now I had forgotten the name of my guest as well. In a fine sweat, I was about to offer my hand in pretence of recognition when I saw what I had taken for a friendly smile was in fact a discomfitting grin. The fellow was grinning as if he could see through me. As if he knew me to be the hypocrite I felt I was.

"Well, here we are," my companion said, with his hand on the door that opened on the dining room.

In the moment's shock I realized I had been the sport of a magician. All the while—some thirty seconds perhaps, at most a minute—I had thought my anonymous acquaintance was approaching me I was approaching myself in a full-length mirror.

The plastic smile, the unnerving grin, the embarrassed, and short-circuited hand of greeting—all were mine.

I had seen myself face to face, and had failed to recognize me.

Know thyself, counselled the Delphic oracle.

Know myself, indeed! I who am such a bundle of contradictions, such a medley of selves each claiming to be the authentic I, the genuine Who!

Which self is sovereign when all are pretenders?

Perhaps the Buddhists know the answer. They tell us there is no permanent self, only an aggregate, and all aggregates are impermanent, "all things are devoid of self." To quote a modern Buddhist: "If from a man you take away his physical form, sensations, perceptions, mental activity and consciousness, what remains? Where will you find the man existing in himself outside corporality and mentality?"

In this context I recently had a moment of illumination afforded me by a five year old, a little boy with his bare feet planted firmly in the actual. For his birthday I had brought him a picture puzzle of an airplane with a photograph of the plane on the cover of the carton showing how the many odd pieces of the puzzle fitted nicely together. He promptly emptied the box, then looking in some bewilderment at the scattered pieces on the floor he exclaimed "but where's the airplane?"

Some time ago I was invited to talk about myself on the Columbia University "Oral History" radio program.

I had looked forward to the experience as a pleasurable exercise in vanity. Instead I found it decidedly humbling. Even as I was talking to the recording machine I grew uncomfortably aware of erasures in the tapes of my memory. But what troubled me especially was not that I was forgetting so much, it was what I remembered amounted to so little.

Was this then all there was to my life? This mindless array of facts and fancies, of prejudices and opinions, of happenings and personalities that surfaced as I reminisced? Where was I in all this regurgitation of the past?

When I read the transcript it seemed like so much "pouring from the emptiness into the void." I felt like the old woman in the English folk tale who suffered an identity crisis when her faithful dog failed to recognize her in her shorn skirt. "Lawks-a mercy me!" she cried. "This be none of I."

But it is, it is I, this improvisation I call my life, and fancy it to be of my own composing. I have lived, I say fondly. But would it not be truer to say I have been lived?

"Are we not all a dream of God," asks Unamuno, "and our prayers soaring heavenward man's means to lull his Maker into deeper sleep, so that He might not of a sudden awake, and stop dreaming us?"

Chapter 1

Michel Eyquem was the most unassuming of men, the least of humbugs, but even he could not resist decorating his family tree. Most of his ancestors, he tells us, were born in the chateau of Montaigne, though actually his father was the first to be born there. And the only one to be buried in the "ancestral vault," adds Marvin Lowenthal in the introduction to his affectionate *Autobiography of Michel de Montaigne*.

"My family were formerly called Eyquem." But Michel himself bore the name of Eyquem more than half his life and dropped it only after his father died. "With dry humor," his 'autobiographer' comments, "he even takes occasion in the *Essays* to mock at people who call themselves after the title of their estate, and at upstarts who buy a family crest. Yet not sixty years before he was born his great-grandfather, a plain bourgeois, had purchased from another bourgeois the little fief, the title, and presumably the coat-of-arms of Montaigne."

I am not so sure about the "dry humor" or that Montaigne's allusion to his forebears was, as Lowenthal suggests, "pure Renaissance, a boast and a fib." I have heard too many boasts and fibs in my day, have committed too many of my own, to settle for "pure Renaissance." What interests me is that so uncommonly honest a man, who wished to see himself without benefit of mirrors, should feel any need to assure us that he not only had ancestors, but that they were also the right kind. But then, as he observed, we are all made up of fragments so shapelessly and strangely assembled that every piece plays its own game. There is as much difference between us and ourselves as between us and others.

If a family tree does not exist for us—though of course it has to be there even for the least of us somewhere in the forest—or if it is not impressive enough to satisfy our sense of self-importance, rather than accept the fact we are all born of common flesh we will invent one. Like the wealthy New York woman who claimed she could trace her line all the way back to Solomon. (Who among the king's numerous wives was involved in the primal transaction, the lady did not say.)

What does pride of ancestry amount to without possessions or, in plain English, money. The older the money—that is, the earlier inherited or stolen—the more it is revered. Money talks, as Michel's great-grandfather might have said (had he been an American).

If one is not so fortunate as to have progenitors with talking money, at least let them be famous enough to impress people. For instance, when I asked my grocer for a loaf of bread on credit I told him I was a Nobel prize laureate and a direct descendant of William Shakespeare. "That will be fifty-nine cents," he said.

Probably I indulge in wiseacreing about family because I have so little family of my own to brag about; I am as apt as any man to denigrate what I lack. The veriest savage must have more awareness of family than I have, a surer sense of the past as present. He has his tribal rituals to serve as collective experience and provide the illusion of continuity. He "belongs." But I who am the American-born son of immigrant Jews, one remove from a Europe I never knew, have only a sense of not belonging, of living in exile from my own past.

"By the waters of Babylon, there we sat down, yea, we wept when we remembered Zion." But what's Zion to me who was born and raised in Babylon?

I never had a great-grandfather. For that matter I never had a grandfather. At least I never saw one such nor heard tell of him.

Am I unique in my total ignorance of grandparents, of who they were and what they looked like and when they lived and where and how, and even what their names were? No, I suppose I am far from unique, though it is cold comfort to realize there must still be some, there must formerly have been many, born like me around the turn of the century of poor parents who were too preoccupied with the business of making a living to impart a knowledge of the past to their children.

Who can blame them? The past was what they had run away from. The past was what they wanted to forget.

I once, and to the best of my memory only once, caught a glimpse of a grandmother, (but whether it was my father's parent or my mother's I have no idea), and the face I saw through a cloud of terror did not belong to the living, it belonged to death.

I was still a toddler when one day my big sister took me by the hand to have "a last look at grandma." I remember a narrow box on a table higher than my head, and myself being lifted by the armpits and kicking and screaming to be let down, in horrid fright of the withered little mummy that lay there with its eyes closed, so still, so white, so threatening.

To this day, some eighty years later, I cannot see an

oblong carton, any box of coffin dimensions, outside a warehouse or on a railway platform or being stowed away in a truck or in the belly of an airplane, without a shudder.

I am firmly resolved never to go to any funeral but my own, and then only under duress.

If only I could ask my parents to tell me of those who begat them. Why did I never—why am I so incurious by nature—that now I might summon their shades or at least imagine their existence? But both father and mother have long since gone to their well-earned rest, and now it is too late.

Too late . . . too late . . . How often have I heard those melancholy words echoing down the corridors of my life?

I don't even know where my parents came from, where they were born. Somewhere in the "old country," but where, in what country? And when? Presumably in the last third of the nineteenth century, but what year? Riga, Latvia, Lithuania, Kovno, Vilna, Courland . . . The names of places, words remembered from childhood, come back to me, but they are not much more meaningful to me now than they were then. Where's Courland, for God's sake, what part of the moon? How many centuries did it take my ancestors to get there? How did the once-upon-a-time daughter of Abraham, my mother, come by her fair northern complexion, her blue eyes, and light brown hair.

As to when my parents came to the new world I can only guess by putting two and two together. Since I reached this planet the first month in the twentieth century and was fifth in line in a family of six children the oldest of whom was probably fourteen or fifteen when I came along, I figure my father's departure for America—or more precisely, his flight from military slavery beyond the land of his birth—must have occurred some time in the eighteen-eighties, the first decade of the massive exodus of east European Jews.

One rainy afternoon, when the boy who became me was rummaging in the cellar of our home in north Philadelphia, he found a battered old carton of books in a cobwebbed corner beyond the coal bin. The year before the cellar had taken a bath because of a faulty drain and the cardboard box was still damp when I dragged it into the light; I could trace the high water mark on its sides. The books were ruined, their bindings warped, their yellowed pages hopelessly smeared and stuck together. Not that this made any difference to me; I couldn't have read them anyway. They smelled old and moldy, foreign like the language they were printed in. Hebrew or Yiddish, I supposed. Disgusted, I threw the sodden remains back into the carton and forgot about them. Until just now when the whole thing came back to me out of nowhere. How alien my family's past had become for me at how early an age.

"Each of us knows," I read half a century later in a column in the *New York Times*, "or would like to know with some accuracy the date when he was born, when his parents were born, when his ancestors came to this country, and so on." Each of us, the article concluded, "has the instinctive need of an individual for orienting himself to reality," else he must suffer "the deep psychic cost of ignorance of one's history."

I am aware of the need and the cost though I pretend indifference. How would it help me to live on better terms with myself, I ask defensively, if I could say my folks came over in the Mayflower instead of in the steerage of a larger ship some years later? Yet I envied my college roommate from Vermont who could say the only member of his family who ever made a name for himself was a great-great grandfather who was hanged in England for stealing sheep. Not everyone could claim so distinguished an ancestor, he said. "My people may not have come to England with William the Conqueror, but they were right there to meet the

Norman when he arrived." (My shaggy, tow-headed, rough-hewn roommate had a shambling gait as if his feet were still mired in Saxon soil! It didn't take much imagining to see him wielding a mean battle-ax at Hastings.)

Some years ago, when I was filling out the application form for a passport, I found myself blocked when I came to the question of my mother's maiden name. I could not for the life of me think what it was, if indeed I had ever really known. Exasperated by what I chose to consider a lapse of memory, I was on the point of writing "Mom" when it occurred to me the bureaucrats in the passport office were not particularly noted for their sense of humor. There was nothing for it but to go home and dig into my old records, such as they were, and they were mostly nonexistent.

Unnatural son! What saddened me was not so much my failure to recall—or, in truth, to realize—my mother's maiden name as my inability to think of her as a maiden at all. All those years I had never thought of her as a woman in her own right, only as a mother, my mom.

When I mentioned the passport incident to a friend he was visibly shocked. "Not remember your own mother's name!" he exclaimed, as if I had committed a sacrilege. I think he pitied the changeling.

The changeling was inclined to feel sorry for himself for having so little sense of attachment to kith and kin, and to blame it on his upbringing. Alas! I was as tenderly nurtured as any child in a large family and allowed to grow up freely without preachment or bondage to the past.

Chapter 2

On the wall, facing my desk, is a rubbing from an ancient stone. It is pre-Columbian, the woman at the museum says, the god of maize. How a Mayan deity came to have the fear-dispelling and boon-bestowing hands of a bodhisattva is a mystery to me. But even more mysterious, he resembles my father. Not only in his aura of forebearance and compassion but in his actual features— the pronounced cheek bones and sunken cheeks, the wide mouth, the arched eyebrows. Especially the brows. My father was a great one in the raised eyebrow department.

Like Hakuin in Paul Reps's *Zen Flesh, Zen Bones*, his response to all manner of assertions was "is that so" which he persisted in rendering, no matter how often I corrected him, "is that all." But perhaps "is that all" was precisely what he meant. A lot of the fuss and bother of life must have seemed to him much ado about nothing.

I quote the delightful story of the Zen master Hakuin who was praised by his neighbors as one leading a pure life.

"A beautiful Japanese girl whose parents owned a food store lived near him. Suddenly, without warning, her parents discovered she was with child. She would not confess who the man was, but after much harassment at last named Hakuin.

"In great anger the parents went to the Master. 'Is that so' was all he would say.

"After the child was born it was brought to Hakuin. By this time he had lost his reputation, which did not trouble him, but he took very good care of the child. He obtained milk from his neighbors and everything the little one needed.

"A year later the girl-mother could stand it no longer. She told her parents the truth—that the real father was a young man who worked in the fish market.

"The mother and father of the girl at once went to Hakuin to ask his forgiveness, to apologize at length, and get the child back. Hakuin was willing. In yielding the child all he said was 'is that so?' "

No Mayan god or Zen master, my father was one of Thoreau's "mass of men who lead lives of quiet desperation." (I suspect the sage of Walden was a member of the club himself.) But I never heard my father complain, much less despair, though there must have been times when the battle seemed too unequal, and for a nonbeliever like himself the game hardly worth the candle.

"I'm not an atheist," he said. "I don't claim to know. I'm an agnostic." How quaint the denial sounds in our computer-enlightened day. How old-fashioned the assertion of his agnosticism. He was a proud and humble man most at home with himself and his books but condemned to a life term of toil and worry to provide for his family. He accepted his karma without argument if not without a lift of the old eyebrows. For all the fetters of circumstance, my father was a singularly free man.

He had been married to my mother—my mother-to-be—for only a short time when, still a youth, he left his native village and temporarily his bride for the land of promise. There he could at least escape the possibility of another pogrom and the certainty of years of servitude in the hay foot, straw foot army of the Czar. He was a socialist in his thinking, as were so many of the Jewish emigrants from Eastern Europe in the final decades of the nineteenth century. (It is interesting to note in this connection that the American Socialist Party reached its maximum strength in the first decade of the twentieth when the immigrant tide was cresting.) My father had no love for czars or militarists—or for demogogues, socialist or otherwise. I remember his comment on the speech of a soapbox orator he had stopped to listen to one Saturday night: "Comrades, let us put our heads together and make a wooden pavement."

When in the radical ardor of my youth I denounced the unholy alliance of patrioteers and profiteers bent on dragging the United States into Europe's war (later known as World War I, or "the war to end war"), he offered no objection. But when I scoffed at the rhetoric of patriotism, and said the flag was only a piece of colored cloth that made men blind to their real situation, he told me with some heat I didn't know what I was talking about.

Smarting under his just rebuke I asked him who he was going to vote for in the presidential election, knowing beforehand what his reply would be. "Eugene Debs," he said. "Who else is there to vote for?"

(Debs, the Socialist Party's candidate and a fearless critic of America's role in the war, was then in jail or headed for prison on a trumped up charge of sedition.)

Some years later, when at the age of twenty-two I was working on the socialist newspaper, the *Call,* I had the opportunity to observe the magnetism of the man. Debs had come into the office apparently unexpectedly and it was extraordinary how the dreary, dusty, workaday atmosphere of the place was illumined by his presence. From my neophyte's desk at the far end of the editorial room, I could see it was not merely a matter of hero worship on the part of the faithful who had gathered around him. Love had entered, and the moment was transformed.

It soon faded with his departure as the office sank back into the routine of the day. The ringing of telephones, the clack of typewriters, the exchange of tired clichés once more prevailed. When I mentioned to the office cynic, who preferred to be known as a realist, the sense of radiance I had felt when the visitor was in the room, the same man whose face only a short while ago was positively glowing when Debs embraced him, remarked: "Oh, he was lit up alright. He likes his booze." Every man his own Judas, I thought.

But I go too far afield. By the end of his first year in America my father had deprived himself enough to be able to send money for his wife's steerage ticket. When she landed at Ellis Island she was carrying their first born in her arms.

With what anxiety, what palpitation he must have awaited the arrival of his girl-bride who was almost a stranger to him, and the baby he had never seen. They had had so little time together, he and she; so many lonely days and longer nights had passed since they had last seen one another.

I can imagine how the sudden sight of her in the swarm of old world folk quickened his heart. How very fetching she must been been with her lovely open face, her voluptuous young body ripe for her man. With what yearning he must have looked forward to seeing her again, what desire to hold her in his arms. What sorrow, too, that for all the opportunities they had dreamt the new world held for them, all the high hopes they had shared, he could offer her only a poor workingman's lot.

I don't know if my father ever felt "uprooted" since he never spoke of it. He was probably too busy coping with the present to indulge in nostalgia for the past. He would have relished the title Frank Sullivan later gave to one of his books: *The Night the Old Nostalgia Burned Down.* But then I wonder if the whole idea of the uprooted and the emotion it engenders has not been more the concern of my own generation than it was of his.

When I was a boy the big idea was America the "melting pot." Madame Liberty with her torch was pictured in the popular imagination as the great-hearted mother who gathered Europe's "huddled masses" to her ample bosom. In reality she took far more than she gave. Our debt to the multitude of those anonymous heroes and heroines who came to her so eager and so trusting is incalculable. Penniless they brought her their immense riches of youth and strength and hope that built a great nation.

By the time I was old enough to be aware of a world outside my skin, the family was far removed from the ghetto, and Yiddish had become mostly a foreign language. I wish it had not been so for surely the ghetto would have provided a richer environment for my childhood than the lower middle-class, gentile neighborhood I grew up in, with its monotonous row of two-story houses standing cheek by jowl and suggesting the narrow, respectable, sterile lives within.

Lest it be thought that by choosing such an environment my father was seeking acceptance as a Wasp—though I don't think the term had yet been invented—I hasten to add that nothing was further removed from his mind. I recall a visitor who accused him of wanting to "pass" as a Christian. He only laughed derisively.

"Ignoramous!" he declared when the man had left. "He wants to pass as a Jew."

"A professional Jew!" he added contemptuously.

In his later days, his older sons and daughters were

employed and could contribute to our welfare. He had settled his family in the "Pennsylvania Dutch" neighborhood of north Philadelphia because it was one of the few quiet residential areas of the city where a man of his very limited means could afford to buy a house. It was near a park and a school for his younger children, and near enough to his "shop," his place of work, for him to reach it by trolley.

I have never been back but I am told the district is now a Black slum. I would not recognize the old tree-lined cobbled street down which each workday early evening would rumble the great wagons loaded with empty beer barrels and drawn by four stout horses on their way home to the brewery and their stable.

In summer days there would be the one horse wagons crammed with fruits and vegetables from the nearby farms. I can still hear the cries of the hucksters: "Fresh straw*berries!* Fresh *peaches,* plums! New *app*les!" In those primitive days to buy fruit by the pound or the dozen was unheard of. You bought a peck or a bushel so filled to the top the vendor had to contain the generous measure with his two hands to keep the overflow from spilling into the street.

And then, the "baker's dozen." Today you get six buns for the price of twelve. Then you found thirteen in the bag you bought at the corner bake shop, one extra to say "thank you, come again."

As for who his neighbors might be, I don't think my father gave a damn. He was not standoffish, merely unapproachable; neighborliness was not one of his virtues. In truth, as I remember them, they were a pretty ignorant lot. They were very provincial, very bigoted, very Protestant people, who must have considered us outsiders. We may not have been Catholics—Negroes, of course, were beyond the pale—but we were Jews, which was almost as bad. Still, we were the "good kind," so it was alright.

My father was a born loner and, as I came to realize, a better educated man than his neighbors. He apparently felt no need to "socialize." He even found it a nuisance, I could tell though only a child, to have to say "good evening" to the neighbor next door whose front porch was separated from ours merely by a wooden railing.

"You might at least talk to him sometimes," my mother said. "He's a human being."

But my father only sighed. "There are so many human beings," he said.

When he came home from work on a summer late afternoon he would go upstairs to wash, put on a clean collarless shirt, and after supper—it was never "dinner" except at midday Sundays—he would come out on the porch where daylight still held, fill his corncob pipe with tobacco from his five-cent pouch of Bull Durham, and settle back in his rocking chair with the evening paper. This was his hour of contentment and he did not intend to spoil it by being neighborly.

He was a bookbinder, a member of one of those almost forgotten craft unions that existed when the century was young. It was a pleasure to see how carefully, one could say almost reverently, he would handle a handsomely bound book. There was still a lot of hand work then in the making of books and a man could take pride in his skills. He could also enjoy an ample lunch free for the price of a nickel beer. "The saloon is the workingman's club," he said. No clubman and no toper, he said he always took a second beer, not because he really wanted it but because he felt one was not enough to pay for his helping from the free lunch counter.

One day I heard him telling my mother the job was not what it used to be; the machines were moving in and with them a new kind of worker. One of these young "louts" had the "nerve" to tell him to his face he was working too fast. Was he trying to make things harder for the rest of them?

"It makes me sick," my father said. "A man needs to be his own boss."

My mother knew what that meant. Twice before he had given up the job to go into business for himself, becoming the proprietor of a small green-grocery store. This meant going to the market before dawn and slaving behind the counter into the night. He also worried about bills, his own and his customers'. It was a killing way to be one's own boss. My father had no mind for business. Both times he had failed and now he was bent on trying again. With another failure there would be nothing for it but to go back to the job, like an old work horse returning to the stable.

Though we were hardly "well off" the odor of poverty never pervaded our home. This was thanks to the fact that by the time I was ten my two older brothers and two older sisters were employed and helping to meet the family's expenses. If there were few luxuries there was always enough to eat—real food, not ersatz embalmed in plastic that lines the shelves of our supermarkets today. There were good enough clothes to wear, a comfortably furnished house, not omitting a victrola and a piano that was the bane of my existence when I had to practice the music lessons my sister tried to teach me.

Yet there must have been hard times, for I can remember being sent to the nearby wholesale bakery for a loaf of "yesterday's bread" which cost three cents instead of five.

And then there was the butcher with his bloodstained apron and topless straw hat that made his bald head, when he bent over the block, look like a full moon rising. When I asked for a pound of the top of the round, "trim the fat and grind twice," and added, "my mother said to charge it," he withered me with the aside, "some people have millionaires' tastes and paupers' pocketbooks." I hated to go to his store but I could not tell my mother why.

Speaking of "charge it," I can still remember the fly-specked sign yellowed with age I saw in my childhood on the grimy wall of the neighborhood cobbler's shop:

> Since man to man is so unjust,
> I hardly know which one to trust.
> I've trusted many to my sorrow,
> So pay today, I'll trust tomorrow.

It was the first poem I ever learned by heart.

My father seemed to have thrown his traditions overboard on the way to the new world, or to have left them behind in the steerage. "Just so much useless baggage," he said. He refused to belong to any synagogue—"I mean 'temple,'" he added. "It sounds more Christian." He did not attend services on the high holy days, though everything in the house had to look brand new for the Passover and he abstained from food on Yom Kippur. When I came of age my mother wanted me to be prepared for Bar Mitzvah, but he would have none of it.

"Let the boy alone," he said. (Or was it "Leave the boy alone"?) "He knows what tribe he comes from, and if he doesn't he'll learn soon enough." I wonder that he took the trouble to have me circumcized, though I feel certain he would never have resorted to giving hygiene as the reason for the operation.

Poor mother! It grieved her that we were not members of a temple where her daughters might find suitable husbands. To live among the "goyim" in our narrow Gentile neighborhood must have been exile for her. As it probably was for my father, though he would never admit it. "Our people managed to survive in the desert," he said.

That he loved my mother I have no doubt, though the certainty does not stem from any obvious show of affection I observed as a child. Except the one I vividly recall through eyes supposedly closed in feverish sleep I saw them leaning cheek-to-cheek over my sick bed, their fond hearts joined in fear lest my illness prove to be one of those childhood dread infections all too familiar in our neighborhood.

What mother and father felt for each other could be quite the devastating opposite of love it sometimes seemed to the little boy who was too young to understand. I am thinking of those moments, fortunately very few and far between, when my parents had heated recourse to the language of their youth. This was perhaps so I would not know what they were saying, but more likely because the emotion that held them captive could not otherwise find expression.

Those dreadful moments of strife between father and mother. To the bewildered child who listened in the next room they seemed suddenly to rise out of nowhere to darken all his horizon, until in terror and anguish he felt his whole world shattered, all security gone forever. How deadly they seemed to the innocent eavesdropper who was yet old enough to be torn by violence that was beyond his comprehension. It was not until later in life, having experienced for myself the ambiguities of married love, that I came to realize how such bitter quarrels, when the dark side of love's moon reveals the tormented face of hate, might be a game of passion that could also be an augury of renewal.

Now I understand, or think I do, what as a child I could not possibly grasp. How a woman, when she senses her man has too long taken her for granted, will use her wiles to play on his vanity, his jealousy, to arouse him to a pitch of fury and thus bring him back to her, and to his own manhood. My mother was all woman, and if intellectually she was no match for her philosophical husband, she had her own female wisdom.

Chapter 3

I listen with some scepticism to those who tell of happenings they experienced in their infancy, and even in the womb. Their memories are plainly not inventions entirely, but they often seem to have been decanted from stories overheard in childhood, family reminiscences and the like.

A friend of mine says he can remember using his loaded diaper for a slingshot as he stood in his crib. A big red rose in the design of the nearby wall paper was his target.

"I couldn't have been much more than a year old at the time . . . I remember distinctly," he added when I seemed dubious, "because suddenly there was my father in the doorway looking on. He had caught me bareassed in the act."

"And what did your father do?" I asked.

"He laughed. As if it was a big joke. I was so surprised. I expected him to be angry and instead he was haw-hawing. Probably that's why I recall the whole thing so vividly. I remember jumping up and down in my crib in sheer glee, I felt so clever. To hear my father tell about it in after years you'd think I had been some kind of infant prodigy."

I wish I could break through, or somehow get behind the screen that hides my earliest experiences from me. I can recall

---

precious little of my life before I was five, so little it is almost as if I had not yet been born. Like any child I must have been bombarded with impressions as necessary for my nourishment as the air I breathed and the food I ate. On the other hand, for a baby—and until I was five I was the baby of the family—I suppose there is no clear distinction between inner and outer. There are only needs real or imagined, needs and satisfactions, or frustrations. I was little more aware of the world that contained me than I had been of the womb on whose fathomless waters I floated dreaming like the god Vishnu.

Sleeping fetus, sleeping man! Why am I so dismayed that I draw a blank when I try to remember my beginnings? Is not the same thing largely true of all my years? Even the most cursory review of my life shows me to be what G. I. Gurdjieff called "sleeping man," one who walks and talks and acts, or rather reacts, in a state of "walking sleep."

In his fascinating book about the enigmatic "G"—*In Search of the Miraculous*—P. D. Ouspensky quotes him as saying: "It is possible to think for a thousand years, it is possible to write whole libraries of books, to create theories by the millions, and all this in sleep, without any possibility of awakening. On the contrary, these books and these theories, written and created in sleep, will merely send others to sleep.

"There is nothing new in the idea of sleep. People have been told, almost since the creation of the world, that they are asleep and that they must awaken. How many times is this said in the Gospels, for instance? 'Awake,' 'Watch,' 'Sleep not.' As long as a man sleeps profoundly and is wholly immersed in dreams he cannot think about the fact that he is asleep."

"As dreamers wake from sleep, we wake from waking," writes the poet, Kathleen Raine. It is probably only those moments when we "wake from waking" that remain with us. All the rest of what we assume to be recollection may be our attempt to "knit up the ravelled sleeve" of memory and thus give the illusion of continuity to what was actually a series of unrelated happenings. Seemingly unrelated, that is, to one another, like fragments of a shattered frieze, though perhaps not to what Virginia Woolf suggests may be the "hidden pattern" in us.

"Every day," says Mrs. Woolf, "includes much more non-being than being . . . It was a good day but the goodness was embedded in a kind of nondescript cotton wool. This is always so. A great part of every day is not lived consciously . . . As a child then my days, just as they do now, contained a large portion of this cotton wool, this non-being. Week after week passed at St. Ives and nothing made any dent upon me. Then, for no reason I know about, there was a sudden, violent shock; something happened so violently I have remembered all my life."

One morning shortly after my fifth birthday my big sister took me by the hand and said, "Let's go upstairs and see your baby brother."

I had no idea what she was talking about, what a baby brother might be. I had never heard of such nor seen one around the house. Dutifully I climbed the stairs, crabwise, one big step at a time, and still clutching my sister's hand timidly entered my mother's bedroom.

Timidly, also apprehensively, for in the hard morning light the room looked unfamiliar. It no longer seemed the comforting haven it was on those Saturday evenings my mother would tuck me in her warm featherbed after she had bathed me. There I would drift off in a cloud of delicious sleep before being carried, still slumbering, to my own bed in the colder room I shared with an older brother.

How remote it all seems now—paradise lost. My mother's quiet embracing laughter when, as she bent over the tub to bathe me, I pointed to my bellybutton and asked what that was for. The sheer sensual delight of curling up in her big double bed after my bath, the feeling of absolute security. And how interesting, how significant I suppose, that I should still speak of my mother's bed, not my father's, not *their* bed.

Why was he home now when ordinarily at this hour he would be away at work? What was he doing standing there at the foot of the bed, and why was he smiling a different kind of smile than I was used to seeing? And my mother, under the covers instead of being up and around the way she always was, with one startling white shoulder and arm showing and her long brown hair all loose and streaming over the pillow? I had never seen her that way before.

She, too, was smiling—but not at me. Her smile was not for me. She was smiling secretly at something she was holding close with its tiny head nestled in her breast.

I stared but did not see. Or rather, with the fatal insight of a child, I saw but dared not look. Completely unprepared for what must have been an instant irreparable sense of loss, I turned away, the dispossessed, fallen from grace.

In retrospect I cannot recall feeling any undue curiosity at the time, or resentment, or jealousy. I was indifferent to the usurper who had taken my place in the kingdom of my mother, and I left the room quietly by myself. The whole experience had sunk immediately to the bottom of my being, not to surface until many a long year had passed.

Overnight I became a "sickly child," something—I gathered from family talk—I had never been before. I lost my appetite and began to suffer from a plague of itchy hives and rashes.

"He must be eating something that doesn't agree with him," the doctor said sagely. "Try changing his diet." But the problem was not what the child was eating, it was what was eating the child. Luckily, little was known then about allergies, so I was not subjected to a series of useless tests. But, oh, the tablespoons of castor oil dumped down my gullet, the sulphur and molasses of the spring months, the pints of citrate of magnesia I had to swallow (and to this day have made champagne distasteful to me).

To account for my condition, which stubbornly resisted all cures, the family had come up with a unique theory, or rather had been offered such by our learned physician. This was perhaps more to satisfy their need for a rational explanation of my symptoms than by way of a medical diagnosis. It seemed I was suffering from "bad blood" caused by faulty immunization, though I had been vaccinated years ago without any noticeably harmful results.

I don't know how long Job was tormented with boils ("try changing his diet") but my ordeal lasted the better part of four years. Then one evening I was once again put to bed early with "a temperature" and a new crop of eminently scratchable pimples on my chest and belly.

It was not measles, the doctor said, definitely it was not measles, proud of his ability to be positive about something. Could it be scarlet fever, my worried parents whispered after he was gone as they examined me on their own. I could understand their fear. At that time the yellow sign the Board of Health required to be pasted on the door of the house of the stricken was enough to frighten anyone.

I could understand their fear but I could not share it. Even scarlet fever was welcome if it made me the focus of their visible distress. With what satisfaction, what positive comfort I observed through half-closed eyes their troubled countenances as they bent over me. After they had tiptoed out of the darkened room and carefully closed the door so as not to make any noise that might disturb me, I hugged my pillow in delight and fell into the blissful sleep of the just and the cunning.

By morning the "temperature" was gone and most of the rash had disappeared. Shortly thereafter my appetite returned as if it had never left home. The "sickly child" had all at once become well again.

Chapter 4

But early wounds cut deep. Presumably healed by time, they can open again in strange ways and unlikely moments.

My conscience still troubles me when I recall how spite showed its ugly face one rainy afternoon when I was playing with my "baby brother" in the bedroom we shared. No longer a baby, the little innocent had reached the ripe age of six and I a corrupt, eleven. (How odd, I have no memory of his existence before then.) We were having a grand pillow fight when, in the midst of all the hilarity, I happened to have my back turned to my opponent and he, the little sneak, struck at me with his pillow.

With what righteous wrath I turned on him—a sudden puritan of the old school. "You lousy bum!" I stormed. (At that time children used more refined language than they do now.) "Hit me when I'm not looking! Just for that you go stand in that corner with your face to the wall!"

If only he hadn't obeyed me. But he did, meekly, with tears streaming down his cheeks, his head bowed in mute reproach. At this my heart smote me and now I too was crying, though I could not know why. So Cain may have wept for the innocent Abel slain by his hand.

It was not until "midway in life's journey" when, as the poet says, I found myself in a dark wood, unable to go on or retreat. I came to have some insight into what had happened to me that morning my sister took me by the hand and said, "Let's go upstairs to see your baby brother."

One night, more to escape from myself than for entertainment, I dropped in to see a movie that was showing at a nondescript theater that I came upon by chance in my wandering of the city streets.

I say "by chance" as if chance was the exceptional in our lives and not the rule. It is written "seek and ye shall find." It is probably true that if we seek hard enough and long enough we will manage somehow to find an answer to our question that satisfies us, even if we have to invent it. Between happenstance and what we like to believe is design, we obviously find the latter more reassuring.

"People seem unable to admit the principle of chance," writes the Japanese author, Shehei Oke, in his scarifying novel, *Fires on the Plain*. "Our spirits are not strong enough to stand the idea of life being a mere succession of chances— the idea, that is, of infinity. Each of us in his individual existence, which is contained between the chance of his birth and the chance of his death, identifies those few incidents that have arisen through what he styles his 'will'; and the thing that emerges consistently from this he calls his 'character,' or again, his 'life.' Thus we contrive to comfort ourselves."

Perhaps I was enticed by the name of the theater—the Averne. Averne . . . Avernus . . . the name seemed so improbable yet appropriate to my mood that I had to read the sign twice to believe it was real. When I came into the theater I saw it was indeed a dark wood. I didn't know what I might find there. The title of the film, its subject, its actors, who had written the script and who directed, what had been said of it in the press, all were unknown to me.

I expected to be bored. Instead I found myself absorbed,

indeed transfixed as I watched the story unfold of a troubled black boy who felt himself unwanted, rejected. Somehow, in ways I could not understand, could only feel, I was deeply involved. I was myself that boy. I was the delinquent in a reform school who finds a friend in one of the guardians, or I should say the guardian finds him, and through loving kindness almost succeeds in restoring him to the human family. But then jealousy, that most consuming form of insecurity, destroys in a moment all that had been so patiently nurtured, and the boy runs away.

At least I think it was jealousy, but it is now more than thirty years since I saw the film and I would not swear that's what it was. What interests me is that jealousy is the word which comes immediately to mind when I try to explain the situation, as if in response to some interior dictation.

I recall the final vivid sequence which so moved me; the long straight railroad tracks streaming to the horizon, the lost child trudging between them. And walking some distance behind him, not hurriedly but with infinite patience, his guardian, his friend who loves him, his "hound of heaven."

To those who recognize the movie I am referring to—I have forgotten the title—and who may be annoyed by liberties my memory may have taken with the story, I suppose I should offer apologies. It has not been my intention to rewrite or edit the original scenario. On the other hand, it would not be the first time I have done just this. Sometimes, on reading again after an interval of many years, a well-remembered passage from a favorite book, I have been struck by the realization I have rewritten the passage in my mind to conform with my own psychic pattern.

I left the dark theater in a daze, impressed, depressed, desperately lonely beyond the bounds of self-pity.

Why did I so identify with that deprived little black boy whose childhood was so different from mine? Especially why had I been so moved by the torn photograph he obviously treasured, presumably the picture of his mother? What made me so certain he had torn it himself, and in such a way as to slash the man who was standing behind her with his back to the camera? Even more perplexing, was I reading into the story something that just wasn't there, subconsciously rearranging details and possibly even inventing to satisfy some inner need of my own.

But I grew weary of playing the amateur analyst, of asking tiresome questions to hide from the answers I already knew. I was no longer thinking of the boy and his mother but of myself and my own mother. How all those years I had shrunk from embracing her who in some remote golden age of my life had been as close to me as my own flesh and spirit. As a young fellow returning home from school for the holidays, and later from college, before entering the house, I would have to steel myself to greet my mother with a show of affection I did not feel, could only guiltily feel the lack of.

Unnatural son! How often I accused myself, yet remained powerless to change. Seeking from other women the embraces I denied her.

I stopped short, confounded by what I now saw plainly for the first time. Unnatural son, indeed! Say, rather, incestuous infant! Rejected lover! Determined beyond my knowing to punish her who had been unfaithful.

Oh dear God! Was it possible a little "innocent," a mere baby, could so deeply resent another in his mother's bed as to carry his vengeful hurt all those years?

"Jealousy cruel as the grave," says the *Song of Songs*. "The arrows thereof are arrows of fire."

Chapter 5

I owe a great deal to my oldest brother, the infant immigrant who came to the new world in his mother's arms. He changed the course of my existence—for better, for worse, who can say? Perhaps I owe most for a recognition of the cost of success. My brother was seduced by the American dream of "upward mobility" and his life was an American tragedy.

He first came into my ken the night of the big fire, playing a violin.

I remember being roused from sleep in my crib and wondering, as I was being hurriedly and unaccountably dressed in the dark, why the window was so red. The building across the street was ablaze and the firemen had alerted the family to be prepared to leave the house if the flames should spread. As I recall, there was an iron fire escape on the side of the building we faced, and there, on the landing level with the second floor window of my bedroom, I would sometimes catch a glimpse of men and women in strange guise. The place was a burlesque theater and they were probably performers enjoying a break in their routines.

After the dark of the bedroom the living room was a sudden oasis of light. Everybody was there—father, mother, older brother, two older sisters—everyone including Bootsie the cat.

And standing in the middle of the room under the chandelier, cheek-to-cheek with his violin, was still another one, a new one to me. I had no awareness of ever having seen him before. It was my other brother, the oldest of the tribe.

Everybody was too intent on the music he was making to take any notice of my being worried about the commotion in the street outside. I was soon asleep again in somebody's lap, but something of what the fiddler was summoning from his violin must have gone through to me. Most of a century has passed since then but even today when I hear a certain passage in the Mendelssohn concerto the whole scene comes back to me larger than life: *Family Portrait, circa 1903.*

The next thing I knew it was morning and sunlight. The fire was no longer there across the street, only black holes where there had been doors and windows before. Water dripped from some of the eyeless sockets down the scorched face of the building.

So nobody had to evacuate after all. "Evacuate"—that was the word most grown-ups used—there had been no need, they said, to evacuate the house. It was a new word and I went around rehearsing it.

If I have no memory of my musician brother before the night of the fire, neither have I after that night until I was sixteen. The years when I was growing up he did not live in the same house as the rest of us, or even at long intervals in the same city. The little I know of his life in those years, and earlier, is compounded of hearsay and surmise. But then, what do we ever really know of anybody's life, our own not excepted, beyond the markers of dates and facts?

According to family legend, my brother had been something of a wunderkind. (I remember coming across a photograph of him as a child—little Lord Fauntleroy, lace collar, finger curls and all, very European—holding a violin by the neck. When he

33

was eleven, a Philadelphia "society lady" wanted to take him with her to Europe where he could continue his studies under a famous master, but my father refused his consent (no doubt much to the relief of my mother who considered her first born quite perfect as he was).

All this, of course, was far away and long ago, before I existed. That my father regretted his decision was plain from the vehemence with which he defended himself in later years. "If the boy had it in him to be a great violinist," he said, "he wouldn't have needed Europe. He would have made it on his own in his own country."

Maybe, but only maybe. My brother's "own country" was really the late nineteenth century Jewish eastern Europe that gave us the Heifitzes and the Elmans in the first decades of the twentieth. This was the cultural fatherland from which he had been exiled as a child to an America that was still musically a backward country. In those days Europe was the only proper launching pad for a young virtuoso.

My father was well aware of this, which is why it so irritated him to be reminded. He himself loved music, and certainly he had no wish to stand in the way of his talented son. Why then did he say no to the "society lady." I thought it must have been his stiffneckedness that made him refuse what he considered charity.

As the protected American offspring of a European father who had sacrificed his own dreams to provide for his growing family, I was too young to understand how need rather than pride might have been the important factor. With four underage children to provide for—two more waiting in the wings—and with steady employment never assured, it was hardly amiss for a worried father to be thinking of the day when his oldest child might be able to help. Anyway the boy was still a kid. Once removed from the fold, who knew what might become of him? The parental concern was genuine even if it was short-sighted.

And so the switch was thrown and a dream derailed. The metamorphosis of a possible artist into an impossible businessman had begun. My brother was scarcely out of his knee pants before he was earning what was called "good money" performing at elegant soirées of the Philadelphia elite. Before he was twenty he had his own string ensemble playing in a posh hotel in Atlantic City during the season, and in Philadelphia after the summer.

He could not long be content simply with "making good money." "Old money" was different, the kind he could sense in the homes of the people he was invited to entertain with his fiddle. "Old money" meant you came from the right family, lived in the right neighborhood, went to the right schools, wore the right clothes, and graduated from the right college.

In the Horatio Alger America of the youth's rising expectations everything was possible. Why should Phil the fiddler not become Phil the financier even if he didn't marry the banker's daughter? Not that my ambitious sibling wanted to be a financier particularly. He just didn't want to remain a "mere fiddler" all his life.

To be a "college man" must have seemed to him a mark of superiority. Today when college graduates are a dime a dozen and a degree the white collar equivalent of a union card, the idea seems quaint. In those provincial times, however, very few on our family's rung of the social ladder could afford to attend a university or even consider such a possibility.

Of course what my brother needed, if he was to go into business and make his fortune as he intended, was less a degree in the humanities than an elementary schooling in shrewdness and how to manipulate his fellow man for profit, both of which qualities were conspicuously lacking in his nature. Notwithstanding, to college he would go, and the college of his choice was Harvard. To him, Harvard must have meant the most, a coveted ticket to the world of "old money" and the right people. Even so, he might have escaped his fate—if anyone ever does—by working for a Ph.D., as one of his academic mentors suggested, with a view to becoming a professor. It would have meant a way of life more congenial to his substance than a career in trade. But he was stubbornly bent on his course.

Before he could hope to enter the sacred precincts of Academe he would have to pass the College Board examinations, a formidable task for one who had not even finished high school some years earlier. No matter. As Mr. Longfellow wrote:

> The heights by great men reached and kept
> Were not attained by sudden flight,
> But they while their companions slept
> Were toiling upward in the night.

He would toil upward in the night to pay for his days of study, and once in college would continue to earn his way with his violin through four more long years of preparation.

I ache to think how many weary nights he must have spent toiling with his fiddle to attain those heights "by great men reached . . ." Apparently he saw no irony in the sacrifice he was making to pursue his dream of success: an accomplished musician who by his nature and training could have played first violin in any distinguished symphony orchestra, self-condemned to hack out jejune tunes in some musical comedy ensemble to pay for his "higher" education.

By the time I was through my second year in high school, he had taken Harvard in his stride and set himself up in business in Boston. The business had something to do with the war boom.

There is nothing so good for making money as a self-righteous war, especially if the killing and the dying are thousands of miles away. Like others riding on the coattails of the "war to end war," my brother, as they say, was making money. Then, not content with having rearranged his own life to his satisfaction, he proceded to rearrange mine.

Why he assumed he had the obligation, or for that matter the right, to play Pygmalion and especially why the family submitted to his will without serious opposition is beyond me. Had we all been asleep these many years, just drifting along on our little isolated cloud until this Jovian visitor came to wake us with his thunderbolts?

Chapter 6

My brother's intentions were of course well-meaning. Or should I say his impulses were? (We call our impulses intentions and credit them with aim but do they not arise from regions anterior to thought?) My brother was an impulsive fellow. For all his hard-earned education he was as mindless as any man who is sure he knows what he is doing and where he is going.

One afternoon in late August of 1916 he blew in from Boston—in those days you didn't fly in on a plane, you blew in on the train—to make two surprising announcements. Surprising to me, that is, though I gathered from the ensuing discussions he had previously hinted in letters home what was on his mind.

His first declaration was that he had changed the family name. Legally, he added, as if that settled everything. Presto changeo, our ancient Hebrew name of Solomon had been cancelled in favor of a New England cognomen. It seemed colorless to me, devoid of resonance, though my brother probably felt it provided the protective coloring he thought he needed for his new incarnation. According to *The Golden Bough*, aging Eskimos sometimes took new names in the belief this gave them a fresh start in life.

I still find it hard to account for my father's seemingly calm acceptance of his son's presumption. As if it was of no importance to him, he merely lifted his old eyebrows and shrugged his tired shoulders. I say acceptance, but indifference is more accurate.

I remember the shock I felt as a child when I saw him, in a sudden and most unfamiliar display of parental wrath, slap the face of this same son, already a grown man in my eyes, for saying something that angered him. Now all he did was shake some tobacco into the bowl of his corncob and strike a match to it as he stood by the window with his head lowered, his back to us.

Maybe he agreed with Romeo—

What's in a name? That which we call a rose
By any other name would smell as sweet.

Maybe he felt that as far as he was concerned it didn't matter. His life belonged to the past. For what there was left of it, he was content to remain the same Mr. Anonymous he had always been. He might even have tried to argue himself into believing that after all it might be better for his offspring to have an American name, a Gentile name.

What's in a name? Perhaps a rose would smell as sweet if called by another name, but how would the rose feel about it? Would it feel a stranger to itself? Suffer an identity crisis? I didn't know then what an identity crisis was. Perhaps it hadn't yet been invented, but thinking since about the event, I can see how it confirmed the sense of estrangement that was already mine in embryo, the feeling of alienation, of being a changeling.

"The question, 'What's in a name?' would seem nonsensical to every person of the ancient Orient," writes Theodor Reik in his book, *Mystery on the Mountain*. "What's in a *name?* Everything . . . The name is part of a person—as essential as part of his body. Without a name the person has no social form or reality; he has given up his identity. The affinity between the pronunciation of the name and the personality is, according to an anthropologist, as certain as a chemical reaction, with the same fatally necessary effects."

Not that I was aware of this as I listened, confused, to the babble of voices around me. What baffles me is the blank I draw even now when I try to recall my reaction. I must have been shaken, but no serious disturbance seems to have registered on the seismograph of my being. It is as if I was only a mute bystander on the edge of the crowd, observing what was going on yet remaining uninvolved. But I was a sensitive youth and the block in my memory suggests a different scenario.

After supper that evening my brother delivered his second message. I should mention that at the time I had a Saturday job pushing a delivery cart for a big fruit and vegetable market in the neighborhood. Nobody had told me to take the job and I didn't see anything unusual about it. It simply seemed the thing to do if I wanted "spending money" for myself. It was just as I took it for granted that the normal thing, when I was finished with high school, would be to get full-time work doing something, (I didn't know what), to earn my living like the rest of the family. Very plebian! But I was a pleb. A dreaming young pleb waiting to be roused in sleep to a different dream. This rousing our visitor from outer space did for me when he snorted "delivery boy." I resented this.

"What's wrong with that?" I flared up, rushing to the defense of the proletariat. Delivery boys of the world, unite! I had become a devoted reader of the *Masses*, the radical bohemian periodical that considered itself as did its susccessor, the *Liberator,* the voice of enlightened socialism.

Each week I would take the trolley downtown to the newsstand that carried the magazine. It was there I became acquainted with Art Young's irreverent sheet, *Good Morning.* Some years later when I met Mr. Young and mentioned I had been a fan of his cartoon magazine, he said: "So you're the one! I always wondered who bought that copy."

What I wanted to ask him and felt too timid to ask was had he really fallen asleep in the courtroom when he was on trial for treason. He was tried along with Max Eastman and other radicals who were so unpatriotic as to question the alleged motives of their government in declaring war. When prodded awake by a guard he was reported to have said, loud enough for the judge to hear: "If you want to hang me alright, but don't push."

However, to return to my big brother, he waived aside my protest on behalf of the working class. He had other plans for me. I was to be sent back to the drawing board and remodelled a Harvard man.

I didn't know then and still am not sure what kind of specimen such a man is supposed to be, but recently I had the opportunity to observe his caricature. It was around four in the afternoon and the bar at the Harvard Club in New York was deserted except for myself and the two men facing me across the room. One was the conventional old school tie, buttoned up, buttoned down, Brooks Brothers undergraduate type; the other, older and somewhat seedier, I thought was probably attending one of the graduate schools, Business or Law or Education or whatever. In any case his appearance did not spell Harvard, he was plainly not a "Harvard man."

"Tell me," he was remarking to his neighbor, "is there any

rule in this club that says two members drinking at the same bar must not speak to one another?"

"Not that I know of," said the Harvard man stiffly, and putting down his half-finished Scotch and soda he left the room.

"Why put ideas in the boy's head?" my father was asking. "He still has two years to go before he even finishes high school."

"I'm not putting any ideas in his head," my brother said, drumming an irritated tattoo on the table. "It's high time he went to a decent school where he can be properly educated."

I hadn't thought my public school was indecent; it was much too ordinary for that. What he had in mind for me, he said, was one of the fine old New England private schools with a record for funneling boys into Ivy League colleges.

I listened with only half an ear, for by now my imagination had caught fire. Adventure beckoned from afar, a different and more colorful life. Suddenly my commonplace existence had become a monotonous plain inhabited by discontent, while before me stretched fields of asphodel.

"And the money?" my father said. "You know . . ."

"I know, I know," my brother broke in, dismissing the question with an impatient wave of his hand.

His rude gesture upset me, and when I saw the flush of anger on my father's face I feared an outburst that would spell disaster. Couldn't the visitor realize he was treading on thin ice?

"Naturally," he said, "I expect to take care of him."

"Naturally," my father echoed sarcastically. Then to my surprise, for he was not much given to quoting, he added quietly, almost as if he was talking to himself, "upon what meat does this our Caesar feed."

My father was a reticent man who never found it easy to say what he felt. However, at that moment, as he looked briefly and searchingly into my eyes and saw I understood yet feared a confrontation, I think he was telling me not to be afraid. His ardent wish was that I might have the kind of life he had at my age thought could be his.

It was one of those moments of recognition you do not forget. There had been another not long before, when we were sitting on the porch in the pleasant warmth of a summer evening. I had been telling him of my discovery of Dostoevsky's *Poor People*. Then I heard my father say gently, "Who knows? Maybe some day you'll be a writer, too," almost with awe, as if to his mind to be a writer was a sacred trust.

"You want . . .?" he said now, questioning me across the table. But I was too moved to say anything.

He rose from his chair with a sigh. Perhaps he remembered when he had refused to let his talented boy be taken to Europe to study under a master and had thus deprived him of what might have been his.

Unhappy, I observed the son observe the father shuffling out of the room. A line I had once read somewhere came back to me: "He was deposed from his kyngly throne." The royal words hardly seemed appropriate for the homely situation, yet I felt I had taken part in an ancient rite of succession. I had seen the "kyng" my father put down by the usurper, his son.

When I think of my brother—and how little of my sojourn in purgatory has been given to thoughts of him—I have a sense of things gone awry, a wasted life. He has been lost now these many years, the victim of misplaced ambition which became, in fact, the cancer that lay waste his body. I think of him in his lonely grave on a suburban hillside and I grieve remembering with what assurance he paid in advance for a barren future.

Life, the original confidence man!

Or is it for myself I grieve who took so much and gave so little.

His several forays into the world of business ended in failure, as had his father's before him. He was not meant for the marketplace. He had a gift for coming into an enterprise whose days of profit were numbered. I recall visiting him in his office in Boston at the beginning of my freshman year. I left with the disheartening conviction it was no go, that behind the busy facade loomed the shadow of frustration and failure. He was trying so hard to make real that he already knew was unreal for him.

By the mid-twenties he was gambling in the stock market, still expecting without hope the unlikely to happen. His marriage had failed and as if pursued by a vengeful fate, he had injured his hand in an automobile accident. Even if he wanted to, he could no longer play his violin which lay buried in its casket. When the market's crash came at the end of the decade what paper profits he thought were his went down the drain.

Like other men of his generation, he never recovered from what was indeed the Great Depression—in more ways than economic. A lonely man living in a furnished room on a side street, his dreams became fantasies, his illusions delusions. They were almost all on the order of schemes for cornering the market in such necessities as electric refrigerators for Eskimoes, or selling millions of pairs of shoes to the Chinese army—laughable if they were not so depressing.

I had not the heart to question him when he would call at my office to tell me about his latest dream of success, ending with a request for a small loan to tide him over until . . . It was a humiliating experience for both of us and, when his office calls became a regular weekly occurrence, a source of irritation I could ill conceal.

The bitter residue is my recognition that I had not compassion enough even to the measure of my shallow understanding. I had not love enough to ease his anguish.

How often I have been tried and found wanting. Oh my brother, when I think of my selfish concerns, when I feel how unfeeling I have been, my ingratitude rises to haunt me.

Purgatory is not hereafter. It is here and now.

Chapter 7

"Have you ever been in Cambridge before?"

My questioner at the breakfast table was a lanky, cadaverous, bespectacled man of uncertain age with a green baize bag bulging with books slung from the knob of his chair, and a voice that seemed to come from some subcellar of his interior.

I shook my head. I had never been in Cambridge before.

"Young man," he said portentously, "you will soon learn that all Cambridge is divided in two parts, Cambridge common and Cambridge preferred."

This apparently struck him as chucklesome, but as I was unfamiliar with the topography of New England towns, not to mention the language of the stock market, all I could do was grin obligingly.

After breakfast that first morning in the boarding house on Oxford Street to which my brother had brought me from Philadelphia the night before, we sallied forth to interviews with the headmasters of several well-known preparatory schools. It was then I had the opportunity to see for myself the difference between the two Cambridges.

These men who had so courteously replied to my brother's request for an interview to see if I might be admitted to their hallowed halls were obviously Cambridge preferred. Were we then, my solicitous brother and I, Cambridge common?

The question occurred to me in the course of our session with one headmaster in particular who frequently consulted his wristwatch, as if to remind us his time was limited. It was the first wristwatch I had ever encountered, and in my "Pennsylvania Dutch" neighborhood's lower middle-class eyes it marked him as a sissy.

He deeply regretted, he said, that unfortunately we were applying too late for admission to the Academy that year, while for the following year there was already a waiting list. That this was true I did not doubt. What bothereed me was his overly affable manner. But even more I resented my brother's obsequious manner, the oleaginous tone of his voice, as if he was standing on his hind legs begging for a favor. It made me squirm with embarrassment.

He finally succeeded in finding a decent school for the ingrate. In fact an excellent school—Newhope Academy. (Let us call it Newhope rather than give its actual name lest in these permissive days my description of its puritanical regime seem libelous.) It then may have been less famous than some of the other preparatory schools in New England, less clannish. There may have been less "old money" around, but in scholarship and discipline it was recognized as second to none.

Especially the discipline. How those in charge of our minds and our bodies managed to keep several hundred maturing boys and randy youths in virginal confinement in a modern industrial city remains a mystery. We students claimed our alma mater put saltpeter in the food to keep our tails down but this may have been only a canard. Our caretakers pooh-poohed the idea.

Breakfast at seven, lights out by ten at night. On weekdays classes were from eight-thirty to one o'clock, and from five to six, with time out in the mornings for chapel. Half a day on Saturdays, church on Sunday. Visits to town limited to one afternoon a week, except for seniors. Smoking without written parental permission and then only at certain afternoon hours in a designated club room was forbidden on pain of being suspended for three weeks. If you left the campus at night, and were caught in the act, you were forthwith expelled.

No band of novices ever had less latitude. If forbidden games were played, as they probably were, they were not visible to my innocent eyes. This was not due to any excess of virtue on my part; my innocence was mostly compounded of ignorance. I was too green to understand readily my fellow students' leering references to the "leaning tower" of Pisa. That was the name of a Latin American youth who was sent home, it was said, for too openly "beating his rod." Nor did I know anything about homosexuality, had never even heard of it. As for girls, perish the thought. Or just perish. It did not occur to me to inquire into the cause of my wet dreams.

Smoking tobacco was something else; you couldn't do that in your sleep. Still, some way had to be found to flout the laws of the monastery. Mine was to puff at a pipe early in the morning, before the housemaster was likely to be awake. If you crouched in the empty fireplace the smoke presumably would go up the flue. As Alice remarked to the dormouse who lived on treacle at the bottom of the treacle well, "I should think you would have been ill." "So I was," said the dormouse, "very ill." But what was a little nausea compared to the delight of defying the established order. I doubt if I would have begun to smoke at sixteen if it had not been forbidden.

My first term at Newhope—with two years of high school to my credit I was enrolled as a junior—I lived alone in what may

have been the only room available at the time of my late enroll-
ment. I had a narrow cot, a book rack, two wooden chairs, and a
battered desk. It was on the ground floor of the oldest of the three
dormitories; the communal bathroom and toilet were a flight up.
The absence of a roommate did not trouble me. I was a solitary by
nature if not by choice. I wouldn't have known what to do with a
roommate.

In spite of my inability to make friends easily, the surprising thing was how readily (for one who had never lived away from
home) I accepted my new environment after the first several
nights of homesickness. But then like a chameleon I always seem
able to adjust to whatever the color of my surroundings. I wonder
if this may be partially due to the age-long experience of my
people who had to accommodate themselves to wherever they
settled in their wanderings and whatever natives and customs
they encountered.

To help my brother pay my tuition and board, I did
various odd jobs around the school: tended the small academy
shop and worked with occasional clean-up crews. But my main
job was to rise at six-thirty each morning and race through the
corridors of the dormitories clanging a cow bell loud enough to
wake the dead. It was not only a duty, it was fun. With what
fiendish glee I imagined, and sometimes heard, the curses of the
sleepers I had so rudely roused.

I can still hear the inevitable grace mumbled by the
headmaster at the far end of the big dining hall while we sat with
bowed heads at our tables before falling on our food. Still hear,
that is, the closing words. (I could never make out the rest of the
prayer which I interpreted as "for Christ's sake, amen," but which
I always heard as "for Chrissake, let's eat.") And the benedictions
of our righteous "prexy" at morning chapel, mixing quotations
from the Bible with admonitions to wash our socks. Of all the

hymns we sang I remember "work for the night is coming when man works no more" as the most depressing. Why work, I thought, if death is your only reward? It didn't seem to make sense. I was sadly lacking in the Protestant ethic.

The schoolboy tricks I learned to play. To bluff was easy, to succeed divine. If I knew my Greek lesson I would pretend to be hiding behind the boy sitting in front of me and thus invite the foxy teacher to catch me presumably unprepared. On the other hand, if I really was unprepared I took care to keep my eager countenance in full view, fairly exuding self-confidence. It usually worked.

Physics was beyond my powers. The instructor's face would grow purple as I stood paralyzed by the blackboard, unable to add O to H^2. Nor was I any more brilliant in chemistry until one day I took it into my head to memorize the twelve pages in our textbook that we had covered since the previous test. I proved myself to be Pasteur junior by getting an A. The shock was too great for our good teacher. That afternoon he collapsed in the street, the victim of a heart attack.

I was better at reading, writing, and learning things "by heart." The assignment was to memorize Milton's *L'Allegro*. When I was summoned in class to continue from where another boy had left off with the lines

> Or whether as some sager say
> Zephyr with Aurora playing
> When he met her once a-Maying   .

I began confidently

> There on beds of violets blue,
> And fresh blown roses washed in dew
> Filled her with . . .

---

at which point I stopped dead, my mind suddenly a blank. "Filled her with . . ." I repeated, perplexed at my inability to continue and aware that some of my classmates were snickering. "Filled her with . . ." I was becoming more and more embarrassed by the growing laughter in the room, "filled her with . . ." Finally the exasperated instructor slammed his book down on his desk.

"Filled her with thee a daughter fair," he shouted. "That's enough! Quiet everybody! Sit down!"

Which I did, thoroughly put down and put out. I attributed my humiliation to the fact I was feverish with a cold. It was not until several days later when I was recuperating in the infirmary that it occurred to me what Zephyr was up to when he was playing with Aurora on beds of violets blue and fresh blown roses washed in dew.

By now our country was at war, but for most of us at school the war was as remote as those we read about in our American history textbook. Not so for our aging athletics instructor who must have fancied himself some kind of military strategist. Like the general in *Mother Goose* he marched his troops up the hill and marched them down again. Poor General, he loved his memory of the Spanish-American War not wisely but too well. He was bent on storming San Juan Hill all over again. The battle was not without its casualty—himself. That night he was in the hospital, in the intensive care ward.

We were obliged to go to the church of our choosing on Sundays. I shopped around at the various worship centers in town, but like the thief who was permitted to choose the tree from which he was to be hanged I could find none that was to my liking. Until one Sunday I had the good fortune to find a Unitarian minister who still occupies a prominent niche in my private pantheon.

51

I should note in passing that if I never thought of gracing a Roman Catholic service with my doubting presence, neither did I think of attending a synagogue. I did not even inquire if there was one available though there were probably several in town. Was it that I preferred to be taken for granted as a Christian because it was the easiest way in a gentile environment? Very likely, and likely too that I would have resented the imputation. Youthful hypocrite, not to have asked if and where I might find a temple, not to have made it clear I was a Jew and as a Jew I felt no ties to any Christian heresy. On Hebrew orthodoxy, I should add.

The austere interior of the Unitarian church I attended was as unpretentious as the outside of the old building; the congregation, largely elderly and as I recall unobstrusively distinguished, seemed to me superior to the ordinary run of churchgoers. I don't think I merely imagined this to be so. The whole atmosphere of the place made palpable the old New England ideal of plain living and high thinking, the New England of Emerson and Thoreau.

But what impressed me most was the person of the minister, an intense man of large dimensions, physical and spiritual, whose face mirrored earnest thought and controlled passion. There was that about him which made me think of the great abolitionist, Theodore Parker, whom I imagined he resembled.

He spoke a beautifully pure English with no trace of the conventional ministerial unction in his voice, and his sermons were free of cant and dubious piety. He would always preface them with numerous quotations not only from the Old Testament and the New but also from the teachings of the Buddha, from the *Bhagavad Gita*, from the writings of Montaigne and Erasmus, Whitman and Melville, whatever he deemed appropriate to his text. In my youthful eyes, he was an ancient prophet in modern dress.

What then was my dismay when one Sunday I gathered from his sermon on civil disobedience that he was not only talking about the idea in general but also about himself in particular.

With patriotism rampant in the wake of war, apparently it was required—by what authority only God knew—that the flag be displayed in the pulpit, and he would not, he said, he could not countenance such a transgression. The state's business and religion's were quite separate, and the one should not be used to support the other. Moreover, in the name of patriotism meant in the name of war, and he was unalterably opposed to war in whatever colors it paraded. As he could not blind himself to the symbolism of the flag he had no choice, he said, but to resign his pastorate.

When he concluded, "So help me God I can do no other," there were tears in his eyes, and they were not tears of self-pity. With his parting words, this stubborn humble man of principle stepped from his pulpit and walked in sorrow down the aisle and out of my Sundays.

All honor to him who laid his convictions on the line and considered no sacrifice too costly for what he believed. He taught me by example what it meant to be serious.

It was a lesson well taught but not as well learned. Many years later, when appearing before a congressional committee, I resorted to sophistry to sidestep a question meant to entrap me, I felt I had failed him as I had failed myself.

Chapter 8

I was against "the war to end war" but not so much I could not do my bit. It was not a matter of patriotism but of cash. In this, how did I think I differed from those "merchants of death" I held in such abhorrence. We were all after the quick buck, bosses and workers alike. And now women, too, appropriating their husbands' and their sons' jobs in the factories.

I needed the money because I needed a tutor to help me get by my college entrance examination in German. And the quickest way I knew of to get some cash was to work in one of those factories that were profiteering from what was called the "war effort." One month of that kind of effort would pay for the next month's tutoring.

Four weeks of aching limbs and swollen hands and deafening noise, feeding a machine that polished small pieces of steel which would eventually become some part of a gun, or of a bomb, or God knew what. I didn't want to think that one day some of these bits of steel might be rending young flesh like my own, making holes for death to enter. Thinking was not one of our college entrance requirements.

What I remember about those sultry August sessions in a deserted school room that followed my month in Hades is not

German grammar. What I remember is the sweet torment it was for me to be sitting next to my teacher on a narrow school bench that contained the two of us like sardines in a can.

She was an attractive young woman—and what young woman was not attractive to me in my state of concupiscence! It was all I could do to contain myself. If I found my leg pressing against hers, or my hand grazed her breast as I hastened to turn a page in our textbook, or her body as she shifted her position in our crowded quarters smote me hip and thigh, I could feel myself so big I did not know how to conceal my engorged stem.

Possibly she was amused by my discomfit, if amused is the right word. Teaching German grammar to an aroused faun armored in proper jacket and necktie on a hot August afternoon could not have been much fun for her, especially when the faun was so plainly embarrassed. However she seemed quite unaware of my agony, or I was too inexperienced to know if she was, despite my dreams of seduction in her absence.

Considering the circumstances, which were hardly conducive to the right kind of concentration, that I managed finally to pass my test was some kind of minor miracle.

When I think of the lunatic roles I have played in the dream theater of my life I am inclined to believe there must indeed be a "divinity that shapes our ends." High on the list of lunacies is my enlisting in the U.S. Army at the outset of my freshman year in college. Never did a more unlikely recruit give promise of becoming a more impossible soldier.

As I came up for air at the Harvard Square subway station in Cambridge that September day of 1918, I had no thought of joining the Army. Yet, when I caught sight of a recruiting center in the immediate vicinity, I proceded to sign up for the duration of the war.

Probably my sudden impulse to volunteer was not as

thoughtless as I like to assume. I was draft bait in any case. As an enlisted student I could attend classes several months free of charge, also enjoy free board and lodging and even a dollar a day, courtesy of Uncle Sam.

I can't say I found very inspiring my brief martial career in the Students Army Training Corps. (The sailors around Boston called us the Saturday Afternoon Tea Club.) I felt absurd, an impersonator in the uniform doled out to me, though I realized it was supposed to stand for something bigger than myself. Whatever that might be, it was certainly too big for my five-feet-two.

Oh, death, where is thy sting, I thought as I stood shivering in line for early morning roll call and had to bark "Here!" when my name was called. Standing next to me was Private Prince So-and-So of the deposed Russian nobility. We were a very democratic bunch in the S.A.T.C. I despised the slick, young second lieutenants who were plainly not sons of our alma mater and took a malicious pleasure in "shaping up" us "Harvard boys." I loathed the endless robot drilling, however necessary it was claimed to be for our own good, and the senseless running around Soldiers Field with rifle and pack until I was ready to drop. Especially I hated bayonet practice with its shouted admonitions from our mentors to "stick it in" the dummy, "stick it in like you meant it." "Get him before he gets you." "Go on, stick it in! Rip his guts out!"

After such enlightened meditation it was hard to stay awake in the classroom while the professor was expatiating on the glories, shall we say, of Chaucer's poetry.

Mercifully I came down with the flu and spent the better part of a month in the infirmary. (I remember with affection the elderly nurse who took care of me and who, when I was well enough to sit up in bed to read and I asked her if the plays of

George Bernard Shaw were available in the library, remarked, "Isn't he rather mature for you?")

The second week in November I was discharged from the infirmary, and shortly thereafter from the Army without having to stick a bayonet in the guts of a single live German. What a relief that was for this battle-scarred veteran of the war to end war.

It's good the American Army wasn't made up of the likes of me. I recall our great "victory march" through the streets of Boston on Armistice Day. A little boy on the sidewalk said as he pointed to me, the "shorty" at the end of a line of sixteen, "Look, Mom, I'm as big as him."

"You little bastard," I thought. "Here, take this goddamn gun. Save it for the next war."

Chapter 9

Until freedom was taken away from me and then restored, I had not realized how precious it was. But it was not until late one afternoon when I escaped from a classroom that I tasted the very *tsimes* of freedom.

How I, a poor student of mathematics at best, came to be studying trigonometry is one more of those unaccountable happenings of my life. Yet there I was, surrounded by hostile logarithms, totally indifferent to what the instructor was scratching on the blackboard with his piece of chalk that kept breaking under the force of his excessive emotion.

Thoroughly bored with what I could not understand and had no wish to, I was sitting there wool-gathering when a voice spake unto me. "Why are you sitting on your hands with your mouth open like a stupid ape?" the voice said. "We make our own prison and contrive to lose the key. Arise and rejoice in thy youth! In short, get the hell out of this wretched mathematics class. It's not for you."

Which I did forthwith, and never have I enjoyed a happier moment than I experienced as I walked out of that room and emerged from the dimly lit corridor to be greeted by the last rays of the setting sun and the wind in my face, a free man. I felt lighter than air. Freedom, says Engels, is the recognition of necessity. It is also the realization of possibility.

Now that I was deprived of the trooper's dollar a day I was in need of what a classmate called "walking around money." When I asked him what that was he explained there were two kinds of money, W.A. and F.K.

"W.A.," he said, was the ordinary garden variety one needed to get by—"walking around money."

"And F.Y.?"

"Ah, that's different. "That's the real thing. F.Y. is fuck you money."

Some years later, when I saw him again in New York, he told me he had worked his way through the Harvard law school by playing "scientific poker."

As I was no good at poker, I had to find some more prosaic source of income for I could not in all conscience continue to depend on my brother to meet my expenses. Now that peace, or what was called peace, was at hand, my financial burden was too much for him to carry. Like other amateur businessmen who had profited in the war years when the government was spending the people's money as if the supply was endless, he lacked the foresight to get out before the postwar recession hit him.

I typed manuscripts for professors, waited on tables in the Union dining room and at parties. In the spring of 1919, I found work serving as a part time, one-man information bureau stationed, without benefit of uniform or chair, in the lobby of the Boston Public Library.

You can always tell spring has come to Boston, a proper Bostonian (from the midwest) explained, when the magnolia trees at the foot of Commonwealth Avenue are in full bloom and covered with ice. One such fine afternoon, while standing at the top of the steps leading up from the street to the library entrance to observe the aftermath of the wedding in the church across the plaza, I became aware of a stranger beside me. He seemed to be a pleasant enough young middle-aged man, if somewhat high strung, well dressed, and very well spoken. I would not have given him a second thought but for his bitter remark when the bridal couple left the church in a hail of rice and flowers.

"Poor fools," he said, "they think they'll be happy."

I thought it was a pretty sour and uncalled for kind of remark but I made no comment. After a spell of conversation, he asked if I would have lunch with him the following day. I was surprised but I gladly accepted his invitation. It was not every day I was offered a free meal.

When I appeared on the appointed hour at the address he had given me he seemed taken aback, as if he had not expected me or had forgotten his invitation, or I was mistaken about the day or the hour. However he quickly regained his composure, said rather nervously, "just a minute," and without asking me in withdrew to get his hat and coat.

In the course of our lunch, he confessed he had not thought I would show up and had almost wished I wouldn't. Curious, I asked him why.

"Oh my dear, do you really want to know?" he said with a show of weariness that struck me as rather put on.

"Well, if you must know . . ." he added, though I was not aware of any urging on my part.

About six months ago, he confessed, he had got into trouble over a boy. "The whole thing was silly, really, much ado about nothing," but he had had to leave town until the thing blew over. His wife had divorced him—"The one good thing in all the bad news"—and he had spent the interval in isolation in Vermont trying to mend his ways. I was the first boy he had approached since his return. (I had not thought I was still a boy.)

My unsuspecting acceptance of him, he declared, had helped to restore his confidence in himself.

I didn't quite understand why he was telling me all this, or even what he was telling me; I was too inexperienced to read between his lines. But I was hungry, the food was excellent, and if he found confession good for his New England soul, that was alright with me. We parted with a warm handshake. "You're very sweet," he said, and he walked off jauntily. I went my way to the library, trying to figure him out and the reason for his confidences which struck me now as probably only half true. I was still green in the ways of the world; indeed, I seem to have been woefully normal.

Several months later, there was the evening I had bought a balcony seat to see Ethel Barrymore in a play whose title I have forgotten and was waiting in the lobby of a nearby hotel for the theater to open. After a while I became aware of what used to be called a portly man observing me from across the lobby. When I met his eye, he gave me an indulgent smile. I thought I probably did look amusing to him, standing there daydreaming with my schoolbooks under my arm, and I shyly returned his smile and left the hotel.

What was my surprise when a little later, as I paused before entering the theater to look at the photographs of various scenes in the drama, to find the same man standing beside me.

"Would you like to see the play?" he asked.

"Oh," I said, "I already have a ticket."

"Good for you," he exclaimed heartily, as if I was to be congratulated for being so thoughtful and, putting his hand on my shoulder, he asked where I was sitting.

"In the balcony," I replied casually. I was beginning to feel annoyed.

"Good God, the balcony!" he exclaimed, dismayed that I

should suffer so from deprivation. "Give me your ticket and I'll exchange it for two good seats in the orchestra. Wouldn't you prefer that?"

Suddenly apprehensive, or driven by some instinct for self-preservation, I took fright and fled from the stranger and from the theater. With my ticket still in my pocket, I was afraid to go back to see the play lest I encounter my new friend.

"That's all there is, there isn't any more," as I understand Miss Barrymore said in the play. I never did get to see it.

Years afterward, when I was reading Proust, I recalled the incident and recognized the intruder with his powdered jowls and painted lips as a kind of bargain-basement incarnation of the Duc de Charlus.

Chapter 10

From my attic window in one of the freshman dormitories, I could see a big tract of vacant land across the Charles River and adjacent to Soldiers Field (where I had recently been training so assiduously to defend my country). When I revisited Harvard some thirty years later, the vacant lot had become the flourishing School of Business Administration: Vatican of the corporations and symbol of the enormous growth of American power in the period between the two world wars.

From the near side of the bridge that "spanned the flood," the School's ivy-encrusted, red brick buildings looked as antique as Harvard Hall, which had been in the Yard before 1776. Certainly they were more in keeping with the historic atmosphere of the college than were some of the faceless modern structures that had sprung up in the neighborhood of the campus. I never did cross the bridge to inspect the plant, but if I had I would not have been surprised to find our future business leaders wearing cap and gown. After all, why not? They were more truly representative of the culture of monopoly capitalism than was my nineteenth century academic class of '22.

That bridge, by the way, had in my time and no doubt still has a bronze plaque imbedded in the pavement to commemorate the fact that a Revolutionary Army officer fell there—Colonel Prescott, if I am not mistaken. "No wonder he fell," an irreverent classmate remarked. "On wet days the damn thing can get so slippery anyone could fall there."

Was I becoming just another old crock so enamored of the past that I could find little good in the present? I wondered about this as I observed the nondescript appearance of the students crossing the Yard. They were those children of the Depression and World War II and Korea, sans necktie, sans jacket, sans everything but a beat-up shirt or sweater, frayed and usually soiled blue jeans, and dirty sneakers.

In my day it would have been unthinkable to attend class in such sorry garb. The story was still current then of a student who had the temerity to attend Copeland's course too informally dressed for the professor's taste. Told to leave the room until he was properly attired, he reappeared before the end of the hour in full evening dress, white tie, tails, and all.

"That's better," Copey said.

What's "better," of course, is what's acceptable. The offending student was simply ahead of his time while the professor, like most of us, was behind. We were strictly World War I survivors. Even the professor's wit, (for which he enjoyed, it seemed to me, an exaggerated reputation), smacked of the well-bred and the well-read.

His comment at the time of the Irish "troubles" was typical. The Union League, whose pro-British sentiments were familiar, was then situated on New York's Fifth Avenue across Fifty-second Street from St. Patrick's cathedral. One Sunday morning after mass, some indignant sons of Erin were in a mood to throw stones. The next morning Professor Copeland asked his students if any of them knew where the Union League was. After several had volunteered information he blandly remarked:

"Wouldn't you say it was just a stone's throw from St. Patrick's."

Old Copey must have felt he had the nod from Oscar Wilde on that one.

The whole world, as one of Sean O'Casey's characters declared, was in a "state of chassis," but we at Harvard in the closing years of the teens and the first of the twenties seemed largely unaware of the extent of the "chassis." Little mention was made in the classroom of the antiradical hysteria sweeping the country—now that we had made the world "safe for democracy."

On January 2, 1920, writes Ray Ginger in *The Bending Cross*, "the Department of Justice raided meetings throughout the country, arresting 2758 men and women, holding 556 for deportation. By the end of January ten thousand persons had been arrested for alleged radicalism, and they were treated with extreme brutality. A revived Ku Klux Klan tortured and murdered throughout the South and Mid-West, with no interference from the police. During 1920 more than sixty Negroes were lynched. Twenty striking miners, peacefully and legally picketing on the public highways near Butte, Montana, were shot down by Anaconda Copper Company guards, and two of them died."

Socialist leader Eugene Debs was in the penitentiary at Atlanta. Sacco and Vanzetti had begun their seven years journey to Calvary, Massachusetts.

In the postwar repression, characterized by the Palmer raids and foreshadowing the age of McCarthy, Harvard's brilliant young professor from England was the target of a vicious attack by the *Lampoon*, the college's allegedly humorous magazine. Harold Laski was pictured as the traditional Jewish monster later to be immortalized in the pages of *Der Sturmer*. He was also seen as the then standard long-haired, wild-whiskered, bomb-carrying, pacifist Anarchist Bolshevik, whatever strange breed that might be. His crime was to have spoken at a meeting of the wives of those

Boston policemen who had dared to strike, and thereby given "cautious Cal" Coolidge, governor of Massachusetts, his big push on the road to the White House.

It was rumored at the time that A. Lawrence Lowell, president of the university, was so incensed by the breach of Harvard etiquette on the part of the magazine's editors—which must have seemed to him almost as bad as a Harvard professor defending a bunch of strikers—that he wanted to expel the miscreants. Laski persuaded him not to. I don't know what truth there was in this rumor. (Later in the decade Dr. Lowell, as one member of the panel of three eminent New Englanders appointed to review the outrageous death sentence of Sacco and Vanzetti, joined the other two in their decision not to refuse the two Italians the courtesy of the electric chair for a crime they had not committed.)

In general our professors appeared to be no more conscious of what was happening outside their classrooms than my teachers at Newhope had been. But then with the self-appointed, attorney-general-anointed watchdogs of our national purity straining at the leash to sink their teeth in heretic flesh, they may simply have considered it wise to remain as invisible as possible.

Perhaps our mentors felt about us the way the Englishman is said to have felt about his bride on their wedding night. "My dear," he chided her, "ladies don't move." All we were supposed to do was lie on our backs with our legs open and get impregnated with culture. But the day of the gentleman scholar, of what might be called surplus culture, was finished, a casualty of the war. Now the stage was set for massman with upraised palm, while in the wings was Spengler's man on horseback (though bomber or gas chamber would have been an apter symbol).

Harold Laski tried his best to make us believe that intelligence was still possible. He once illustrated, for the benefit of our class in English history, the difference between intelligence and mere knowledge of facts.

There was the Oxford student, he said, whose aim was to attend the Divinity School. He had learned that for years a standard question in the entrance examination was: "Who were the kings of Israel?" To be fully prepared, he rehearsed the names and dates of the kings until he could give the list backward as well as forward. Unfortunately the question had been changed that year to "Who were the minor prophets of Israel?" Hopelessly at a loss for the answer he wrote: "Far be it from me to distinguish between the major and the minor prophets of Israel, but the kings were as follows." According to Laski the examiners were so impressed by the young man's intelligence they had no hesitation about giving him a passing grade.

Speaking of Oxford, Kirsop Lake, another of our professors, told us of the time he had tutored candidate theologians at Oxford. One day a student came to him with a note from the dean of the Divinity School. "Dear Mr. Lake," the note said, "I understand you do not believe in miracles. If you can get this chap into Divinity you will have to change your mind."

Laski himself was one of the most intelligent men I have ever encountered. He was a small, slight, thoroughly scrubbed fellow who wore his hat pulled down to his ears and looked no older than his students. He began his English history class by parking his feet in the bottom drawer of his desk—hoping to keep them warm I suppose. Sitting thus sideways, he would proceed to lecture for the next fifty minutes without a break and without benefit of notes, in the most perfect sentences, paragraphs, and chapters imaginable. Sometimes he would end his formal discourse, as if he had finished the last page and closed the book, with the question: "Anybody got a cigarette?"

When it came time to study the rebellion of the American

colonies, he called on several students whose names suggested that their ancestors might have been involved in the signing of the Declaration of Independence. With a few simple questions having to do with the security of the state, he soon had them not only accusing their forebears of having acted unlawfully, but even indicting them for treason and inferring they should have been hanged as traitors.

"Dear me," sighed Laski. "How fortunate they weren't, or you might not be here to condemn them."

He reminded us of what Benjamin Franklin or some other worthy is supposed to have said to his fellow signers of the Declaration: They had better all hang together or they might all hang separately. Laski then went on to ask if any of us American pragmatists had ever heard of a legal revolution.

"Isn't it rather," he said, "a matter of success or failure? If a rebellion is successful it's a glorious revolution; but if it fails, it's a crime against the state."

"Which of course it is," he added, "according to the state."

One morning he brought a book to class, a rare enough occurrence for us to wonder what it might be since he normally spoke without notes or reference to books.

"A colleague," he said, obviously pleased, "Professor Bab bitt, sent me a copy of his new book," and held it up for us to see. "It's titled *Rousseau and Romanticism,* though it has little to do with either. You might enjoy reading it. I did."

Irving Babbitt, when I took his course in criticism the following year, was equally pleased to call our attention to a new book. "By a former pupil of mine," he explained with gruff pride. "Tommy Eliot. *The Sacred Wood.* The new criticism, no doubt."

Another time he showed us a magnificent Renaissance volume, beautifully printed and bound. "You will note," he said (as we passed the book around so all could admire the fine bookmaking and some pretend to read the Latin) "the excellent paper they used in those days. A book was meant to endure. That's what makes me hopeful about so many of our contemporary volumes."

As I considered myself a radical and the "humanism" of Irving Babbitt reactionary, if anybody had suggested I take his course, I would have spurned the idea. Nevertheless I found myself one day asking his permission to enroll. Why, I really can't say. Perhaps I was curious, or considered it a challenge to take a course meant for graduate students.

Babbitt had no objection. He merely shrugged. "It's supposed to be for graduates," he growled. "Still, if you want to study with us, why not."

When I listened to his lectures, I soon came to value the range and depth of his learning. It occurred to me he might have been amused putting a skeptical kitten in the same basket as his faithful copycats. It seemed to me he did not have too high regard for those future pedants among us who were working for their Ph.D., their professor's union card. They were so busy filling their notebooks with their leader's information and opinions that they had little time to weigh what he was saying.

A few years later when I was talking to Van Wyck Brooks in his office at the *Freeman*—he was then literary editor of that excellent weekly, and I was looking for books to review—he told me that he too was a Babbitt alumnus. I asked him what he got out of the course and he said "a notebook of wonderful quotes."

Irving Babbitt was a scholar with considerable knowledge of the classic literature of the East as well as of the West. On my visits to the periodical room of the Widener Library, I would sometimes find him there thumbing through the latest issues of a number of learned journals, pawing their pages like a bear searching for honey. My freshman notion of him as a reactionary was sophomoric. He saw, certainly much earlier than I did and much more clearly, the increasing degradation of language and custom in our democratic Tower of Babel.

True, my revised opinion may be due to the professor's probably amused acceptance of my attempt to pass as intelligent. The big question on our final examination paper was: "Write something about Aristotle's *Ethics*." (He liked to put his questions that way.) I didn't know enough about my own ethics let alone Aristotle's.

I wrote it was useless to talk about the philosopher's *Ethics* without taking into account his society and the culture not only of his time and place in general but also of his class in particular. Aristotle, I said, warming to my argument, lived and taught in a master-slave society where there was one law for the masters and another for the slaves. His *Ethics* being the product of his society and his class could not be other than it was. In short, I wrote what I thought was a Marxist interpretation of Aristotle's thesis without ever touching on the thesis itself.

The fact was I had not read *Capital* any more than I had *Ethics*. My ignorance was appalling, it pervaded every nook and cranny of my education. Maybe Babbitt was entertained by my bluff, or maybe he found what I had written a relief after his scholars' regurgitation of what he had fed them.

Why did I come to have such admiration for a professor to whose conservative convictions I considered myself opposed? I think it was less because of what he taught (though he was an exceptional teacher indeed, a genuine awakener of thought), than of what he was, a man who earned respect without ever asking for it. Anyone could have opinions, but to have convictions was something else again.

Of my other professors, I remember fondly George Lyman Kittredge with his knowledge of Shakespeare and his tyrannical schoolmaster ways. One cough too many in the classroom—he seldom permitted more than three—and he would pick up hat and stick from his desk and stride from the room.

And charming Bliss Perry with his survey of the nineteenth century novel in the old *Atlantic Monthly* nineteenth century tradition of polite letters. And John Livingston Lowes whose book on Coleridge's sources for *The Ancient Mariner* was such a magnificent work of scholarly detection. I took his course on the English romantic poets twice, if only once by choice, because the first time I was so in love with Anna Karenina I forgot it was examination day and I missed my test.

When I told the professor the cause of my default, he said that was delightful but not so much that I wouldn't have to take the course all over again if I wanted the credit. "Only next time," he advised, "don't get lost in *War and Peace*. You might miss two tests."

Ah, Anna Karenina! Tolstoy in his Calvinist phase may have dismissed your story as an "abomination," but you were my first great love. How I suffered for you in your doomed passion for Vronsky. And when at last in your despair, with the angel of death in the guise of a gimpy railroad worker hovering near, you threw yourself under the train, I was inconsolable, I wept for you. I left the library, where I had spent all day in your adorable presence, with my head bowed so others might not see my tears, might not deprive me of the enjoyment of my grief.

I wanted to write, like Tolstoy of course, and Turgenev, and Dostoevsky, and Chekhov, whose volumes I devoured in translation instead of my textbooks, and I vowed that I too would write some day. But tomorrow, not today. Today I would read.

Meanwhile I didn't want anybody to teach me how to write, so I shunned Copeland's course in composition and the literary soirees in his quarters attended by the faithful. The litterateurs who contributed to the college journal, the *Advocate*, seemed too effete to me. Like Theodore Dreiser who would twist his handkerchief and exclaim "yellow nineties stuff" by way of condemning any story or novel he did not approve of, I had little use for refined style. Still, reading his important books, I could not help thinking they might have benefited from an occasional injection of what he so scornfully dismissed as "fine writing."

Chapter 11

In those days Kali, the devouring mother, was the prevailing American deity (as she still is in large measure). To have a girlfriend spend the night in your dormitory room, or the day for that matter, was not merely unacceptable, it was unthinkable. Even to have a female visit you in respectable hours required special dispensation, a fixed time limit, a chaperone, the door to your room left discreetly open. Not that we weren't trusted by our alma mater to behave like neuters, but you could never tell, there just might be some vile seducer among us who would take advantage of an innocent maiden. Such items as sexual permissiveness, sexual freedom, and the like were reserved for a later if not noticeably happier American day.

You may have heard of the English provincial who announced to his cronies at the village pub that he was going to Paris to see if life there was what it was cracked up to be. Questioned on his return about what he had learned in the French capitol he pondered a long moment, then sagely remarked: "Well, all I can tell you is that with us fucking is still in its infancy."

As it was for me and for many of my fellow students who were similarly retarded. There was no Kinsey, no Masters, no sex

73

manuals, no porno films, no course in the curriculum on the theory and practice of cohabitation. Years after I was married (at the ripe age of twenty-two), I still kept it a guilty secret that I had never been to bed with a woman before my wedding night, until I heard other men of my generation confess that they too had been virgin bridegrooms. To a European I suppose such an admission from an allegedly adult male would have been cause for hilarity, if indeed it did not seem too incredible for laughter.

On the other hand, it cannot be said that the age of promiscuity has produced a less fouled-up generation, as witness our sorry record of unhappy marriages and unnecessary divorces. It would seem that something more than our sexual parts is involved in any meaningful man-woman relationship.

No doubt there was plenty of professional service available in the streets of Boston and Cambridge, but I had never been properly introduced; the truth was I didn't recognize a whore when I saw one. If I could blush, I would blush now to tell of my sole encounter with a lady of the evening who picked me up, though I a raw freshman thought it was the other way around. It happened in the night shadows of the Boston Common where I was looking, probably, for the Iseult of my dreams.

Irish, but definitely no Iseult, she was a heavyset frump old enough to be my mother, as I saw to my dismay when we left the Common for the lights of Tremont Street. I felt embarrassed to be seen with her and wished I could somehow rid myself of her company. Too much the little gentleman to tell her to get lost, I suggested we take in a movie where I hoped I would be less visible. When we had settled in our seats in the dim cave and I felt her meaty hand grope for mine I shrank from the touch of her flesh.

Dreading to be seen when the lights came on, I complained of a headache and made her leave the theater with me just as true love was about to declare itself on the screen. Then, still the reluctant gentleman, I escorted her home—an interminable journey in the subway, an agony of self-consciousness as I imagined the other passengers observing us curiously—and beat a hasty retreat without even thinking to pay the woman for her profitless hours with me.

We forget what we might well wish to remember and remember what we would gladly forget. Even the fondest memory cannot bring the past to life again, only nostalgia, only regret.

I am thinking of Marguerite. She who in the long long ago I was infatuated with and who, even after we had been friends for some time, I continued to address as Mrs. Wilde, as if the difference in our age required the formality. Dear Marguerite, dear beloved ghost. Can this be all that is left of my passion of yesteryear?

We chanced to meet in an old Beacon Street brownstone turned rooming house, one of those relics of a more gracious day, where I had dined with my brother and assorted strangers. I recall that after dinner there was music in the front room of the second floor. My brother had been coaxed to bring his violin out of hiding despite his protest that he was much too rusty, and there was someone at the piano. I had managed to escape to the library in the rear whose tall windows gave on the esplanade, with the Charles River beyond.

Not that I wasn't fond of music. I wouldn't take any course that had a Friday afternoon session; my Friday afternoons were reserved for the Boston Symphony Orchestra concerts. (If you waited in line for the box office to open you could get a seat in the second balcony for only twenty-five cents.) But it was not Friday now and it was not afternoon. It was night and it was spring, and I was young and filled with longing. My cup was running over with what poets have called a nameless desire, though what I was feeling was not as nameless as all that.

The books in the library were mostly Victorian sets of the classics. There were also some contemporary works whose publication dates suggested that history must have come to an end around the time of the sinking of the Titanic. The pictures on the wall, which included a signed photograph of Theodore Roosevelt in his Rough Rider costume, suggested an even earlier date.

Among all these dusty treasures, I discovered a volume of Maeterlinck—no prize to the literary snob I was then, but still something to read—and was soon lost in the mists of Cocaigne when a burst of music from the front room came to my rescue. Looking up from my book I saw an attractive woman standing in the doorway. No creature of fantasy but an actual warm body, she seemed to hesitate a moment, as if surprised to find me sitting there, then closed the door softly on the music and came toward me.

I am tempted to add "as the curtain rises." It is all so much like a set piece in the conventional theater of the time that I have to reassure myself I am not making things up, and my visitor and I were not actors in a situation comedy—romantic youth falls in love with older woman at first sight.

Falls in love indeed! Sexually starved, I was dry tinder awaiting the match.

"Am I disturbing you?" she asked.

"Not at all," I protested, rising book in hand from my chair.

"You seemed so absorbed in your book."

"No, no, really. I was hoping you would come."

"Me?"

"Yes, of course you. Who else, since you are here?"

"Charming!"

But I thought it was she who was altogether charming with her ready laughter, her slightly husky voice, her spirited body as firm and slender as a girl's.

"I was afraid to say anything to you at dinner," she said. "You looked so grim. In fact, like the Brothers Grimm."

"You mean you were actually *there*!" I exclaimed, mortified that I could have been so blind as not to have noticed this lovely creature in our boring company at table. "And I never even *saw* you?"

My naiveté seemed much to amuse her, and when I looked pained she laughed.

"No, please don't be hurt," she said, laying her hand lightly on my arm to soothe my ruffled vanity. "Somebody was sitting between us, a dreadful bore, so I couldn't see you either . . . Why are we standing? Do let's sit down."

She seated herself in the chair facing mine and, crossing her legs, searched in her bag for a cigarette which I hastened to light for her.

"Thank you. It was pretty dull, I mean the dinner, didn't you think?"

But I was incapable of thinking anything beyond how shapely her legs were, and when she half turned in her chair to flick the ash from her cigarette, how her small breasts pressed against the white silken stuff of her blouse. And her mouth! I dwelt on those lips as if I had never seen a woman's mouth before. How exquisite it would have been to be swallowed by such a delicious mouth!

"What were you reading?" she asked, pulling at her skirt to cover her knees.

I held up the book for her to see.

"Oh, Maeterlinck!" she cried. "Peleas and Melisande! Don't you just love it?"

Silly woman. So that's what she was really like. She just loved Peleas and Melisande.

"It's been so long," she sighed. "Won't you just read me a bit?"

With a shrug intended to show I could not share her rapture I began to read, only to break off after a few pages when I saw her smother a yawn. I closed the book with an angry bang.

"I'm sorry," she said contritely. "I didn't sleep very well last night and I suppose . . ." She rose and went over to the window.

Instantly all sympathy and even compassion—what games we play—I followed to where she stood in shadow gazing dreamily on the night and the river.

"What, no moon!" I said, moving closer to her behind my screen of sophomoric irony. "The stage directions call for at least a full moon." But she seemed hardly aware of my presence, not even when my hand found itself holding hers.

"How lovely the quiet," she sighed, not withdrawing her hand, and when I said, "especially after the music . . . or was it the Maeterlinck?" she laughed quietly and squeezed my fingers.

Then I did what I thought I had not the courage to do, and would not have had if I was not beyond thought, I turned to her and kissed her. Tentatively, shall we say?

"Umm," she said, as if she had tasted something that pleased her palate, and emboldened by my success I threw myself on her and kissed her again, only this time with all the ardor of pent up desire.

"My, my," she said, freeing herself from my embrace. "Aren't you the impetuous one."

Leaving the window for the circle of lamplight, she rummaged in her bag for her compact, and as she proceeded to work on her face and her hair I observed she was not as young as I had supposed.

"Now I must get back to the gang," she said, flashing me a conspiratorial smile.

Only when I was returning to Cambridge that night in a cloud of euphoria—on foot, I was too high to think of taking the subway—did it occur to me I had no idea where I might find my lady again, or even what her name was.

She called me late the following afternoon on the pay station phone in the dormitory hallway, courtesy of a classmate who yelled my name and "dame here wants you."

"Hello," the dame said. "This is the Marguerite Wilde detective agency. Are you the party who left last night without saying goodbye?"

Marguerite Wilde! So that was her name. Marguerite! Exciting name.

"Oh, Mrs. Wilde, I've been thinking of you all day. Wondering how I would find you. How did you know where I was?"

"We always get our man. I thought maybe if you have nothing better to do this evening you might want to share a little steak with me, and a baked potato."

"Would I! A little steak, a baked potato, and thou . . ."

"Silly." She gave me her address. "Shall we say then around seven-thirty?"

And so it was our affair began. At least I suppose that's what I may call it, an affair, even though it failed to satisfy all the standard requirements.

We would meet several evenings a week for "a little dinner" Marguerite prepared in her modest Back Bay apartment, and for dessert we would make love. Or rather I would make love to my hostess. She permitted me liberties—or invited them—I would not have dared to take had I not been out of my mind with lust, and she could hardly be said to have resisted.

That was as far as our lovemaking ever got, a kind of antic bundling without benefit of couch or bed. There were times when my sweet torment became a desperate trial, when wild with desire as I fondled her in my lap I could no longer contain myself and would suffer agonies of embarassment. She never seemed to notice anything unusual about what now I can only call my waking wet dreams, though it was impossible for her not to have been aware of what was happening.

Marguerite was considerably older than her green lover. She had a daughter almost my age, now conveniently away from home at some finishing school in Connecticut. As a widow or a divorced woman—I was too preoccupied with her present to ask about her past and she never spoke of it—she could not have been so inexperienced as not to know what my passionate caresses were all about. In sober truth I didn't really know myself. I thought I was madly in love when what I wanted was a good healthy fuck.

What I didn't know about women would fill a book and I had yet to learn how to read. But perhaps what Marguerite didn't know about herself would fill another book. Despite her advantage in years and previous marriage, she was in some ways as immature as I was, or almost as retarded. Was she frigid? Had she ever had an orgasm? I was not yet mature enough man to think such questions much less ask them. The impression that remains with me is that we behaved like two adolescents.

Ah yes, there are tears for things, even if in retrospect. What we once took so seriously can become the stuff of comedy.

There was a moment our last evening together—unbelievable, two years had passed since we first met—when having completed my studies in midterm, I was due to leave Cambridge for New York. There was a moment when our strange relationship might have come into bloom, however briefly, instead of being left to wither in memory. It was the moment when Marguerite sighed as if in resignation, went into the next room, and lay down on her bed.

I followed her and sat on the bed beside her and, uncertain at which end to begin to undress a woman first, took off her shoes and then began to unbutton her blouse, when I heard a key in the lock and the front door burst open.

It was her daughter, all tears and runny nose. She had taken leave of her school to quarrel with her beau in Boston and had then run home to mother to tell all. She was too sunk in her misery to notice the presence of a stranger in her mother's bedroom. There was nothing for it but to excuse myself and bid my love a decorous if sorrowful farewell at the door.

Dear Marguerite, you didn't seem too rueful to me. As I remember the occasion you looked rather amused.

Chapter 12

In January the century was twenty-two years old and so was I, but neither the century nor I had any idea of where we were going. Time and chance would tell; they always did when the future became the past. Meanwhile, as I had enough credits for my degree, I felt I should take my final examinations at midterm instead of waiting until the end of the school year. It was high time I learned to walk on my own two feet instead of using my big brother as a crutch.

The day before I said goodbye to Cambridge I had a letter from the Dean's office informing me I had passed my finals among the first ten in my class. Had I made the proper application, the letter said, I would have been eligible for honors. At least now, some sixty years later, I think I had such a message from the Dean, but I wouldn't want to swear to it. Maybe I just imagined the whole thing, the way in my personal age of anxiety I used to dream I never did graduate as I claimed and now the secret was out and everybody would know I was a fraud.

At my time of life, one can't always distinguish between fact and fancy; old men, like poets and priests, may not be intentional liars. "It is unbelievable," wrote Francois Mauriac at eighty, "how little we retain of all that has been poured in throughout all those years. Facts are forgotten or have grown muddled."

Anyway, what good honors would have done me I don't know, unless I intended to pursue an academic career, which I didn't. I was no scholar and no pursuer, I was only an appreciator. I had taken every appreciation course in the curriculum—appreciation of art, appreciation of music, appreciation of poetry. I would have taken appreciation of appreciation if such a course were available.

So there I was—poorly equipped for the marketplace—on the train bound for the "city of opportunity," as the announcer for the municipal radio station characterized New York. "The city of opportunity where eight million people live in peace and harmony, enjoying the benefits of democracy" (as witness the approximately seventeen hundred murders among the thousands of other crimes committed in the same city the year this chapter is written). There I was on my way to the "big apple" with only the vaguest idea, in truth no idea at all, of how I was going to live when I got there, or what I was going to do for a living.

How did one go about finding just a plain ordinary job, let alone planning a career? The veriest dolt was better prepared in that department than I was who had too long been dependent on others for direction. Educated as a gentleman, I was a son of the working class who had lost touch with reality.

For a brief while I tried teaching in a boys school upstate. Or rather, I was tried, and found wanting. The school was a military academy whose academic distinction was notable for its absence. I was hired to teach English and elementary French. My knowledge of the latter was certainly elementary, but I figured a little homework at night would see me through the next morning's class honorably enough.

My uniformed students were also uninformed, though

not much more so than their "professors" who bullied their young charges in the name of discipline. They reminded me of the shavetails who used to torment us "Harvard boys" in the Students Army Training Corps.

The headmaster was the proprietor of the academy. In his portly eminence he looked more like a town banker than a pedagogue. When I reported for duty he issued three orders: first, get a haircut; second, be more military; third, get out. These orders, of course, were issued serially with intervals between, but as I held the job for only two months before I was fired, they seem in retrospect to have followed one another in fairly rapid succession.

The occasion for the third and final command arose at my last supper. Each instructor presided over a table of twelve disciples. When one evening at dinner I was called to the telephone, my band of the faithful made an incredible shambles of our table. I could not have been gone more than five minutes, but when I returned I was horrified to see what havoc the youthful yahoos had wrought in my absence.

All was quiet now as they sat cowed under the baleful eye of the headmaster who was waiting rigid by their side for me to reappear. Then and there he proceeded to dress me down like a drill sergeant in the presence of the entire school. I left the room with my tail between my legs, unaware that fortune had smiled on me, was indeed probably holding its sides laughing.

Back in the city, what to do, where to turn. In my search for a job I was like the little ball in a pinball machine, shuttling from pillar to post in its blind odyssey. After my fiasco at the military academy I was in no mood to try teaching again. Time and chance decided I was to become a publicity man instead.

It was quite the thing, in the early twenties, for fundraisers to employ the high-pressure sales techniques of the recent "war effort" to raise money for the "growth needs" of colleges, hospitals and other worthy institutions. Somehow I managed to find employment in the publicity department of one of these outfits. And because the boss and I were sons of the same alma mater, I was given the munificent salary of fifteen dollars a week. I shudder to think what it might have been were I not a Harvard man.

All through that lonely, hot New York summer I subsisted on a roll and coffee for breakfast and a "hot plate" for dinner (a gray unsavory mess you could manage to get down and hold on to if you were young enough and hungry enough). I have forgotten the name of the joint I patronized but not its proud slogan, which I read as "No worse food at any price." That, combined with my three-dollars-a-week, airless-conditioned hall bedroom on the edge of Greenwich Village near the Ninth Avenue El, made it an altogether memorable summer to forget.

But I was learning something about being a publicity man. On a loftier level, roughly about ten thousand dollars a year loftier, you became Director of Public Relations. Still further afflated, you could become an "engineer of public consent," own you own firm, and even contrive for some backwater college to give you an honorary degree. Years later I recognized the apotheosis of such an engineer in Herr Goebels, the Nazi Minister of Information.

One day I was sent on a mission to Washington to pick up a list of names and addresses from some government department; evidently the list could not be entrusted to the mails. When I returned to the office the following morning, mission completed, and gave the bookkeeper what was left of the expense money he had given me to pay for my trip to Washington, he looked at me as if he was unable to understand such strange behavior. "Young man," he sagely remarked, "you'll never be a success in this business."

He proved to be prophetic. At the summer's end I plucked up enough courage to ask for a raise of five dollars a week and was promptly let go.

And so I was unemployed, and not a moment too soon. If I was not ready to hear a different drummer, I certainly was not content with the drummer I had been hearing of late.

I had for some years been a reader of the *New Republic.* Now I thought I might try my hand at writing for "them." Reviewing books, for instance. Hell, I challenged myself, if I can't earn fifteen dollars a week as a book reviewer instead of as a publicity con man, I might as well fold my tent and quietly steal away.

To me the *New Republic* meant Walter Lippmann whose clear thinking and clean writing I admired. I knew he was no longer an editor of that magazine, he was now a factor on the liberal morning newspaper, the *World.* I asked one of the elevator operators in the old *World* building where I might find Mr. Lippmann. It never occurred to me that I might need an appointment to see him. At twenty-two one does things he might hesitate to do later in life.

"Top floor," the elevator man said, but when I reached the end of the ride and stepped out into the corridor I saw an iron stairway. I climbed the stairs and came to an open door. There behind a cluttered desk sat Mr. Lippmann busily writing what I supposed was his editorial for the following morning. He looked up, seemed startled by my suddenly materializing in the quiet of his sanctuary, and obviously annoyed said, "How did you get up here?"

"Walked up," I said. "I saw the stairs and just walked up."

86

"I see," Mr. Lippmann said, not too testily I thought, considering my flippant reply.

I apologized for interrupting his work, and he said, "What is it you want?"

I said I wanted to review books for the *New Republic*. My simple charm must have disarmed him, for he leaned back in his chair and smiled frostily. He explained that I was not only in the wrong pew but in the wrong church, that in any case he was the wrong person. He suggested that I see Robert Littell who was book review editor of the magazine.

I told Mr. Littell that Walter Lippmann had sent me, which was stretching things a bit, but I was catching on. I was learning that truth can be flexible. Later that day, when I called on John Macy at the *Nation*, I had no hesitation about recommending myself to him as a reviewer for the *New Republic*, although as yet I had not even opened the book Mr. Littell had assigned me.

The next day I saw Albert Jay Nock at the *Freeman*, that comparatively new weekly whose plain good writing was not afraid to mean what it said, which was perhaps too unusual for it to continue publication very long. Mr. Nock, kindly soul, looked as if he had just returned from an awfully good lunch. When I told him what I was after he put his arm around my shoulders, led me to his crowded bookshelves, and said, "What would you like to review?" I felt that in his generous mood he would have given me the whole outfit if that would make me happy. However, on second thought, he suggested I talk to Van Wyck Brooks who was the magazine's literary editor.

It was Gilbert Seldes, then managing editor of the *Dial*, who told me how to be a high-priced writer. Each month the *Dial* published a number of unsigned brief reviews varying in length from fifty to two hundred words. "We pay fifty dollars a piece,"

Mr. Seldes explained. "If your ambition is to become a dollar-a-word author, all you have to do is limit your review to fifty words."

My only signed piece for the *Dial* was on a book sent me by poet-editor Marianne Moore several years later. I forget what the book was, but I remember trying to make my prose as obscure and idiosyncratic as some of Miss Moore's poems seemed to me. I succeeded so well that, when I read my review in print, I wasn't surer of what I read than I had been when I wrote it. But I am being unkind to Miss Moore for the fun of it. I think some of her lines are memorable, some even adorable. One of my favorites is "to be liked by you would be a calamity."

Kenneth Burke, who was assistant editor of the *Dial* at the time, said Miss Moore was so considerate of an author's feelings that, though she might be refusing his manuscript, her letter was still a model of courtesy. "Dear Mr. So-and-So," she would write. "We have read your story with much enjoyment and are returning it herewith."

Burke recalled the occasion when Miss Moore sent him the manuscript of a submission she wanted to publish. There was one thing about it that troubled her, as she explained in her memorandum. She felt the author's use of the word "damn" was in bad taste. Had Burke any suggestion? After due deliberation he replied: "Let's go the whole hog and print the damn word."

It was said that Scofield Thayer and James Watson, the two wealthy men who owned the *Dial* and were its first editors in its reincarnation as a distinguished literary journal, could not always agree on what should or should not go in a particular issue. To settle things amicably, they would resort to trade-offs. Thus Watson might agree to their publishing a piece by an obscure Rumanian author if Thayer would accept some new poems by, say, William Carlos Williams.

One nice thing about being rich is that you can afford your lunacies. I recall an incredible story Slater Brown told me about a taxi ride up Fifth Avenue that he shared with Thayer in the days when the *Dial* publisher was having a wordy duel with the wealthy art collector of Arjurol fame.

Suddenly Thayer ordered the driver to stop. "Let's get out of here," he said, opening the door in panic.

"You know Barnes is out to get me," he explained as they continued their way up the avenue on foot. "That cab driver looked suspicious to me."

Slater at first thought Thayer was putting him on, but soon he realized his companion was deadly serious. He tried to convince Thayer that his fears were unfounded. "After all," he said, "Barnes couldn't possibly know what taxi you were using, or at what hour of the day or night. He could hardly afford to hire every cab in the city every twenty-four hours just to get you."

"Humph!" Thayer grunted. "That's how much you know." He had it all figured out in dollars and cents—so many taxis at so much per driver per hour, including tips.

"Wouldn't that take an awful lot money?" Slater said.

"Money!" said Thayer. "What's money to a man as loaded as Barnes?"

Chapter 13

How did I come to succeed Joseph Freeman as publicity man for the American Civil Liberties Union? I haven't the vaguest idea. But then, what does it matter? Let's just say that's where I was when I found me, as Sally Benson said of the man in one of her many *New Yorker* stories.

The story began, if I remember what Sally told me, with the man standing by an upstairs window. Editor Harold Ross, always a stickler for facts, sent it back to her with the marginal query: "How did he get there?"

"How should I know?" she replied in a marginal note of her own when she returned the script to Ross. "That's where he was when I found him."

The author of *Junior Miss* was responsible for a sketch of mine appearing in the *New Yorker* after it had been rejected by the editors. "What's wrong with it?" I asked her. When she had read the piece she said, "There's only one thing I can see. You have the boy in your story eating a chocolate bar. That's not specific enough for the *New Yorker*. If you said he was eating an O'Henry bar . . . Here, let me have it." She wrote in the change and put the script in her bag.

I'm inclined to believe it was Sally Benson, rather than the O'Henry bar, that changed the editorial mind.

When I reported for work my first day with the Civil Liberties Union, I found a crudely drawn cartoon on the desk in my cubby hole (that had been Joe Freeman's). It pictured a group of doddering octogenarians disintegrating at a conference table. The caption read: "We are unalterably opposed to birth control."

I took this to be the previous occupant's comment on the effectiveness of many liberal causes. As a communist, Joe had not much use for liberals. He probably considered them too ineffectual, too much talk and too little action.

Not that there was much ineffectual about liberal Roger Baldwin and his Civil Liberties Union. Today the A.C.L.U. is a national institution but I still think of it as Roger's own and see it in terms of his modest little office on lower Fifth Avenue where he piloted his cause through the shoals and rapids of the savage postwar repression.

He was a hard-headed idealist in the tradition of Thoreau. He had everything it takes to be a big success in business or politics or whatever, except that he was too honest, a serious fault in any one pursuing a public career. Instead he chose to run a tight little shop—and pennywise he could be plenty tight—dedicated to the proposition that the Bill of Rights was the Magna Charta of the American people and any infringement on its provisions was impermissable.

He held that every citizen—white, black, red, or yellow, communist or capitalist, Ku Kluxer or Daughter of the American Revolution—should be free to write and to speak as he or she chose, within the provisions of the law, if the law squared with the Bill of Rights.

Roger Baldwin was a puritan not given to compromise

with the devil in the name of accommodation. I admired him, though our temperaments were never quite at ease with one another. He was too close-fisted to suit my nature, and no doubt I was too feckless for his. It was therefore with some hesitation that I told him one morning I wanted to take a few days off to get married.

He said I was crazy. Of course I resented his remark, but he was right. Both my lady and I were indeed crazy with the madness of young people in love with love. Neither of us was ready for the marriage bed with its responsibilities and privileges. It was imperious nature that called the tune we heard as the music of the spheres. Not very original of us, but then we were hardly unique.

Maybe in Elysium two could live as cheaply as one but in New York it was difficult. We could not very well make do with the twenty-five dollars a week I was earning at my part-time job plus an occasional bonus from a book review.

At this point my hypothetical reader might be tempted to ask: "Why didn't you look for full-time work that paid an adequate salary?"

Why indeed! What a dunderhead I must have been, how positively un-American, not to seek a permanent position with an assured future, not to make money, to save, to invest, to accumulate, and all the rest of it. "Go to the ant, thou sluggard." Or was it the squirrel whose ways I should "consider and be wise?"

When it came to emulating the ant or the squirrel, my beautiful bride was as impractical, as unacquisitive as I was. Nevertheless we were happy. We would never be happier than we were then, trying to obey Mother Nature's injunction to increase and multiply.

Like Micawber, I was confident something would turn up. One day a stranger introduced himself on the telephone as Bill

Soskin, city editor (or was it managing editor) of the *Call*. The *Call* was New York's, and as far as I knew the nation's, only English language socialist daily newspaper. The paper, it seemed to me, suffered from an excess of dullness. Politically it was as proper as the *New York Times,* as conventional as the Socialist Party had become.

What he was calling to ask, Soskin said, was how did I feel about selling my bourgeois soul to the socialists for thirty-five bucks a week. I said even if the *Call* was a "capitalist tool" . . .

If the *Call* had actually been such I would never have had the opportunity to express myself in print so freely on so many things I knew so little about. Probably management was too concerned with its own approaching dissolution to care what I did.

One day when I was ruminating on the throne in the men's room, I saw one of my columns much trod upon and mired in the muck on the floor. The lesson was not lost on me. This, I thought, is what pride goeth before.

I have always relished the anecdote attributed to a popular novelist about her exchange with the janitor of the apartment house where she had recently become a tenant.

"I see you're a writer," he remarked when they chanced to meet in the hallway outside her door.

"Yes, I am," she said, quite pleased with his recognition. "How did you know?"

"Oh, I could tell," he said. "I could tell from your trash."

To get back to the Civil Liberties Union, it continued to occupy my mornings. After this, I would commute from my clean if dingy office on lower Fifth Avenue to the somewhat less clean and dingier offices of the *Call* on nearby Fourth Avenue.

The publicity man's dream is the item that is so "newsworthy" he doesn't have to go to the press with any follow-up

---

story, the press comes to him. My particular item turned out to be the opening shot in what became the famous "monkey trial" of the twenties.

The tale told of old King Canute may not be true, that he tried to command the tide to go only so far and no further, but apparently the Fundamentalist lawmakers of the state of Tennessee felt they could out-Canute the king. They decreed that Darwin's theory of evolution contradicted what the Bible said about the origin of the species. Therefore it was illegal to mention Darwin or his theory in any public school in the state. (Unbelievable, yet hardly more so than the Volstead Act of the same decade, which made it illegal for Americans to drink anything stronger than soda pop.)

The Civil Liberties Union sponsored a brief statement to the press offering to provide legal defense for any teacher who would discuss the Darwinian heresy in any public school in Tennessee. That was all that was needed to start things moving, the way a loose pebble can start an avalanche.

When a teacher named Scopes offered himself as a test case and we sent word of this to the paper, there was little more to do than sit back and answer the telephone. The newspapers were hungry for a happening to stimulate circulation in a dull summer. The happening was inflated and continued to balloon until it became the circus of the decade, the great Clarence Darrow–William Jennings Bryan debate that was Darwin's finest hour.

The whole thing calls to mind the closing lines of Southey's *Battle of Blenheim*. Old Kaspar is telling the story of the stupendous battle to "little Peterkin" and his friends, and when at last Peterkin asks Kaspar "what good came of it?"

> "Why that I cannot tell," said he,
> But 'twas a famous victory."

I never did know who won the Darrow-Bryan battle, but, after the twenties, I took it for granted that the author of *Origin of the Species* was no longer considered in Tennessee to be the son of Belial. Today I am not so sure. Old Fundamentalists never die, neither do they fade away. Most recently they were demanding that God be given equal time with Darwin in any radio or television discussion of the theory of evolution.

Chapter 14

The golden age of mediocrity, otherwise known as normalcy, was now sailing under full canvas, confidently steering for the reefs ahead. Day by day in every way we were getting better and better. The postwar recession was over; prosperity was just around the corner. With a chicken in every pot, two cars in every garage, and "every man a king" the sky was the limit.

But the *Call* was failing. Had I been more knowledgeable, I might have realized the paper was already on its last legs when I went to work for it. It was ailing like its parent, the American Socialist Party. If either the paper or the party still seemed to be breathing, it could only have been through force of habit.

In his biography of Eugene Debs, *The Bending Cross*, Ray Ginger reminds us that the party's right-wing leaders had "hurriedly disassociated themselves from the Russian Bolsheviks during 1918 and many of them shifted to a tacit support of the war effort." At the end of the war these same leaders still controlled party policies. When their reformist program was challenged by the party's considerable left-wing faction, they retaliated by expelling all individuals and groups who opposed them in the name of "party unity," which is what they accused the Bolsheviks of doing in Russia. The outcome was the "final disintegration" of the Socialist Party in the United States and the advent of the Communist Party in 1919.

To offset the "communist menace" (also referred to as the "communist threat" and the "communist conspiracy"), some of New York's more politically minded unions and their liberal friends promoted the idea of a labor paper to replace the *Call*. The new paper was to be nonparty, published solely in the interest of progressive American labor. The formerly partisan *Call* was sent to the dry cleaners and came back very clean and very dry as the liberal *Leader*. It had almost the same staff as before and reform socialist Norman Thomas as editor-in-chief. The more things change the more they remain the same.

Regardless of politics, the *Leader* was destined to be short-lived and to sink without leaving a trace. It was doomed for the same reason that a number of other newspapers in the country in the twenties (some of which had been around long before the *Leader* was born and none of which could be considered socialist or pro-labor) either had to quit or were able to continue only under combined mastheads. They could not compete with the new media of radio and television in providing information and entertainment for the masses. (This is not to mention advertising, the tail that wagged the dog in any case.)

Times had changed, and with them the audience. The United States after the first world war was not the same country as the young giant that had forded the Atlantic to make the world "safe for democracy." (Nor was it the image its citizens mistook for reality when they looked in the Hollywood mirror.)

Now, instead of newspaper readers, there were viewers and listeners. The conventional paper could no longer satisfy the appetites of an audience that had become audiovisual-minded and no longer depended on the printed word. Witness the popularity of the new tabloids whose millions of "readers" didn't even have to know how to read. We assumed illiteracy had been kicked out the back door, but it was returning through the front. With few exceptions, a literate press was becoming a thing of the past.

Determined not to be old-fashioned, the *Leader* tried what it could not afford, to bring its readers the same complete bill of fare—from soup to nuts—as its capitalist competitors. An up-to-the-minute sports page, for example. The new sports editor did such a good job covering baseball's world series that it just about bankrupted the paper. At least so it was rumored among the staff, although this may only have been an intramural joke.

In any event, it would have taken more than a sports page to rescue the *Leader* from oblivion. The paper was suffering not so much from lack of funds, though no doubt they were inadequate, as from lack of soul. It simply had no valid excuse for continuing to live. True, in this it did not differ from most of its capitalist competitors, but they at least had a clearly defined purpose—to make a profit by upholding the status quo.

By the time I woke up to the fact that our ship was sinking, it had already sunk and so was I. Sunk without a job, which alone guaranteed a dependent man the right to eat. In those antediluvian days, there was no such thing as unemployment insurance or welfare or any other of those "socialist frills." If you were out of work you were out of luck, that's all. Until your luck changed and you were granted the right to eat again.

Mine changed when one day I found myself in the publicity—beg pardon, I mean the public relations—department of the great Edison Company that sold electricity to the citizens of New York. Devil only knows how I got there, or what I had done to deserve such a fate.

There were six of us writers sharing the same office. A

seventh, our manager, had an office all to himself. The department was the special province of the company's vice president in charge of "commercial relations" and existed, as far as I could see, for his glorification. An important part of the publicity manager's role, (aside from providing variations of the vice president's standard speech to business groups, which the manager had written in the first place) was to see to it that the name of the boss appeared in whatever "news stories" and "feature articles" we concocted for the press.

What an unenlightened, unquestioning, unprotesting bunch of white collar slaves we seemed to me, and I one of their number, to accept what I felt was our useless existence as the norm. Was this then what we meant when we wrote about the "American way of life?"

I demurred. I may not have known what I wanted but I knew what I didn't want and that was to go on being a company man. The thought of continuing to work at a meaningless job for a weekly paycheck so that I might work the following week for the next paycheck struck me as bordering on insanity. Such an existence might be satisfactory for a hamster, but not for a man.

It was in this barren field that my first book, *The Company*, took root, and that I was able to express my sense of personal frustration in my first published story, "The Jew," though I was not ready to write story or book for some years to come.

I didn't know I was not ready. Had I known, I don't think I would have had the courage to write to Mr. Kahn. "Where ignorance is bliss 'tis folly to be wise."

I had heard that Otto Kahn, the banker, sometimes came to the aid of artists and writers who needed money to continue their work—Hart Crane, for one, whom I had met recently. Not that for a moment I was under any illusion I was the creative equal of that extraordinary poet. But one day, feeling more desperate than usual, I sat down at my desk in the office and addressed a letter to Maecenas.

I wrote that I needed five hundred dollars to quit my job and get on with the writing of a book I had in mind. Truthfully I had only a hazy notion of what the book might be, or of how far the sum I was asking for might carry a man and his wife even if they lived frugally somewhere outside the city. I may have been fond, I surely was, but I was not bluffing; the intention was honest, the inner need real. I signed the letter and sent it off before I might suffer a loss of confidence. That came later in the day when I was suddenly shocked by thought—a rare occurrence—into awareness of my presumption.

Three mornings later I received an invitation from Mr. Kahn to have lunch with him at the Bankers Club.

The lunch was elegant. It was served in a private dining room, and my host was generous in his attention. He listened patiently to what I told him about my "background" and my "plans" for the future. As we walked back to his office where I took my leave, he said it was not that he gave so much as that others who could well afford it gave so little. He did not say anything about the money I had asked for.

The next day's mail brought me his check folded in a handwritten note wishing me well.

Chapter 15

With Mr. Kahn's check our fortune and our pockets full of dreams, we left New York in the autumn of 1923 bound for Eden, unaware the garden had been closed to the public for some years. Had we been older and hopefully wiser, we might have heeded the sign: "Warning! No trespassing under penalty of the law."

As Adam and Eve, we walked hand-in-hand in the garden, two children who had not yet eaten of the fruit of the Tree. The world was still full of promises. My God! Now in the winter of my days, I tremble to think how young we were, how vulnerable. I want to throw my arms around them to protect them from life.

Eden was then an artists' colony in the Catskills. There we found a two-storied frame house on the outskirts of the village, which rented for a modest twenty-five dollars a month furnished. The house was small, but after our cramped quarters in the city, it seemed wonderfully roomy with its upstairs as well as downstairs. And a real wood-burning fireplace. And curtains! Curtains!

If there was no electricity, we could manage with oil lamps; no gas, the battered kerosene stove in the kitchen would do; no running water, there was a pump outside; no toilet, how quaint to have an old-fashioned outdoor privy down a woodsy lane. That the house was not equipped for winter use did not occur to us city-dwellers in the mild autumn months. With the onset of frigid weather, we could have been as frozen as the pump outside had not a concerned neighbor come to our rescue one bitter January morning of snow and ice and transplanted us in the snug little apartment attached to his barn studio.

But now it was October when Solomon in all his glory could not have been more splendidly attired than were the surrounding mountains. The dry sundrenched days had been touched by the magic of the cool crisp nights. Beginning at the top of the hills, each day more and more of an incredibly beautiful and intricately patterned carpet was unrolled under a cloudless blue sky. How grand, how breathtaking, nature's pageantry of death.

Eleven thinly populated miles from the nearest city, and without the present state road running through the village, Eden was not then the busy place it is now. A number of well-known American artists lived and worked there; with the advent of autumn, some had already left for their studios in New York. Gradually the native vegetation ceased to imitate the local school of painting, and the population shrank to its original proportions of a quiet mountain hamlet.

For those outsiders who remained, finding a model in the winter months could be something of a problem to judge from a story that was going the rounds at the time. One of the artists had finally found a village maiden who would do and he had hired her with her mother's permission and his agreeing not to ask to girl to pose "naked, I mean without any clothes on." When she had sat for him several hours the first day, he suggested they take a break. He asked his model if she would like to lie down for a few minutes. "No, no!" she protested, alarmed. "I don't want to lay down. My mother told me never to lay down for an artist."

Another painter I came to know gave me an unintentional lesson in the creative process. The first day I visited him in his studio he was working on a landscape; the next time the landscape had become a flower arrangement, and the next a bowl of fruit. After several months of labor he finally found what he had been looking for all along. The landscape, the flowers, the fruit had become a beautifully felt portrait of his little daughter.

At the time I was struggling to write what I thought was a novel. I would end the day at my typewriter in a cloud of euphoria, only to begin the next morning considerably cast down as I read what I had written the day before and found it unsatisfactory, contrived. It was no use; I was still not ready. When at last spring came, I consigned my manuscript to the wastebasket.

What a relief that was! There's nothing like releasing oneself from a self-imposed obligation to give the captive a taste of freedom. I should have learned my lesson when I walked out of that wretched trigonometry class, but I'm a slow learner.

I had an interesting dream. Somehow I had managed to fall from a high window in a multistoried building. It's all over with me, I thought as I was falling. And then suddenly it occurred to me that I didn't have to fall *down;* I could just as well fall *up.* And this, to my considerable relief, I found possible to do. I rose until I reached the window from which I had fallen, where with prodigious effort I hoisted myself up over the ledge and back into the room. I was in a great sweat but safe at last.

The fact remained that my cash flow was at the freezing point, and I feared I would have to return to the city to find myself another office job. Then once again fortune smiled on me.

This time it was in the guise of a gracious woman who

seemed to float rather than to walk on this earth, and whose loosed lemon-colored hair and airy gown made me think of her as a figure in a pre-Raphaelite painting. She asked if I would care to teach a class of older children in her little Montessori school in the woods. Would I accept, as part of a necessarily small salary, the use of the cottage on her property, a few minutes' walk from the school on the neighboring hillside?

The cottage was a large, high-ceilinged room with an adjoining, fully equipped kitchen. The wall at the far end of the living room was on runners so it could be rolled open to the trees beyond and the whispering of leaves and the songs of birds. In the moon's light, it did not take too much imagination to think one had come upon the enchanted forest of Arden. In the garden to one side of the cottage, there was a long, hand-crafted table of pine boards between two great evergreens and a bench to match on either side of the table.

It was late in May and summer was bustin' out all over. My class met each weekday morning under a leafy canopy outside the one-room schoolhouse where my pre-Raphaelite lady taught the younger children . . . It was composed of eight or nine girls on the threshold of puberty, daughters of the local artists and the prettiest bunch of posies an impressionable young fellow could ever hope to find.

I should have been content with my good fortune, but characteristically I wasn't. Four and twenty years and nothing done for immortality! One day, as I was crossing the road that led from the schoolhouse to my new home, I suddenly decided to edit and publish my own little magazine, "little" meaning a noncommercial, literary, more or less periodic publication.

"Suddenly" is right (on the spur of the moment), but instead of saying "I decided," I should say I had an impulse, or I had a notion. I can only envy those men of destiny who always know what they are doing and where they are going and can therefore truly be said to "decide." Like Napoleon before Waterloo, to cite a notable instance, or Hitler throwing a fit when his generals had their doubts about the wisdom of invading Russia, or the Japanese warlords planning to attack Pearl Harbor. "Be sure you're right, then go ahead."

I would call my foolhardy venture *1924*, for the year of publication. In my euphoric mood I thought there might even be a *1925* to follow.

By what token an unknown like myself might expect contributions of the quality I wanted to publish I had no idea, or how I was to pay for the enterprise in general when I had difficulty in meeting my grocer's and butcher's bills. Did I suppose that because I expected no payment for my own time and effort everyone else, including the printer, would be of the same mind? The printer wasn't, though somehow I managed to bring out four numbers before he cried enough. No Maecenas he.

In a letter of Ezra Pound's that I came across years later, he refers to me as "one of those who seemed to make some sense," or words to that effect. I must admit, though, I didn't see much sense in the piece he sent me on the music of George Antheil, still less in his subsequently becoming a propagandist for Mussolini.

Poet and novelist Isidor Schneider, who was then advertising manager for the publishing house of Horace Liveright, helped *1924* to come out with a second issue by giving me a full-page advertisement for Liveright books. In the thirties, some time after the original firm had closed its doors, Schneider's literary career was given the deep freeze treatment when, on returning from a sojourn in the Soviet Union, he was thoughtless enough to write favorably about the Communist "experiment" instead of condemning it. Had he chosen the latter course, he would have been welcomed as an authority, just as a decade later all doors were open to those Stalinists who had become anti-Stalinists. He might even have become an editor of *Life* instead of the *New Masses*. Had not communist ideologue Whittaker Chambers succeeded handsomely by jumping from the *New Masses* to *Time?*

To Schneider I owe several anecdotes about Horace Liveright, the foremost American publisher of the twenties, which are perhaps worth a footnote in the annals of our literature.

In his early days as the publisher's advertising man, Schneider learned to steer his copy between the Scylla of "good story" and the Charybdis of "great literature." If he veered to the former, "Oh Isidor," Liveright protested, "you say it's a good story but what does that mean? There are only so many good stories in the world. Is it great literature? That's what people want to know." On the other hand, if he set his course for literature, Liveright despaired. "Who cares if it's great literature?" he said. Is it a good *story?* That's what interests people."

Schneider's second initiation in the mysterics of book publishing involved him as a poet. The publisher had in hand a manuscript of verse written by an emphatically good-looking woman and he wanted to know what his house poet thought of her. "Not much," Isidor reported. "In fact, terrible." Then noting that Liveright didn't seem exactly pleased, he said: "Look, Horace, you know so many beautiful women. Why spoil your list with such tripe just because one of them has a notion she can write poetry?"

"So that's why you think I want to publish her book," Liveright said, with a smile of pity for his naive questioner. "That just goes to show how little you know. This woman happens to be the mistress of the hottest guy on Wall Street and I need the tips."

"Tell you what I'll do," he added as an afterthought. "You want me to publish Robinson Jeffers. You tell me he's a great poet. Okay, I'll publish his book if you'll let me take on this lady's."

"As if," Schneider remarked when he told me this tale, "I had any choice. But at least I helped to get Jeffers published."

The third anecdote is somewhat more philosophical, having to do with the question of happiness. One morning Liveright summoned Schneider to his office. "Isidor," he said, "you're a happy man, aren't you? No, don't deny it. Everybody says you're a happy man. What I want to know is what makes you happy."

Schneider was nonplussed. "Golly, I don't know," he said. "I haven't thought much about it. I guess maybe if I seem happy it's because I was married recently and I love my wife. Then, I like to . . ." He was about to say he liked to write but on quick second thought decided not to lest Liveright get the idea he was writing on the boss's time. "I like to read," he said. And . . ."

"So you like to read," Liveright interrupted.

"Oh yes," Schneider confessed. "So much, it's almost a vice with me."

"That's it!" Liveright declared, slapping his desk for emphasis. And then softly, talking to himself as if his visitor was no longer present. "He likes to read. He enjoys reading. Reading makes him happy."

The next morning Schneider was summoned again to the front office. With a half-finished bottle of bromo-seltzer on his desk and an open bottle of aspirin pills. Liveright seemed to be suffering from a bad hangover.

"Did you give me a bum steer," he growled.

Schneider was puzzled. "I?" He couldn't recall having given Liveright any steer, bum or otherwise.

"Didn't you tell me reading made you happy?"

"Well, yes . . . but . . ."

"So when I got home I started to read. I cancelled two dates I had for the evening. No, I was determined to take your advice. I read for an hour. I read for an hour and a half, Jesus Christ! How long is a man supposed to read? By then it was too late to do anything. I had a miserable dinner by myself at some joint and picked up a chippy. Imagine it, me, Liveright, having to pick up a chippy. And what's the result? I've never felt worse in my life. Is that what you call *happiness!*"

Chapter 16

I had dismissed my class for the day and was about to leave for home when I saw her come into the sunlight from the shadowy interior of the schoolroom. She stood for a moment framed in the doorway—a long-legged, sturdy child whose golden hair and eyes the blue of her middy made me think of summer seas and distant horizons. Then she moved to get her bicycle that was leaning against a tree.

"I'm Elsa," she said in response to my greeting. "I expect I'll be coming here in the fall when we return from Europe."

Her slow, low-pitched voice, her grave inward gaze struck me as foreign.

"I've never seen you around the village," I said. "Perhaps you don't live here."

"Oh yes," she said. "The big house on the hill. When we're in America, that is."

"You are an American, aren't you?"

"Swedish. My parents are American."

I suppose I looked puzzled.

"Adopted," she said. And with that she was off, coasting down the path that led to the road, her hair a golden banner in the wind.

I did not see her again until midautumn when she joined my group. Our humble school in the woods had closed its doors and I was living in a larger house where the class I had inherited could be accommodated.

I had fallen in love with Elsa at first sight. Second sight did not disillusion me. She was lovelier than I had remembered. I watched her come into the room with that remote air which seemed native to her. She was not so much haughty as seeming to guard more secret life. I felt drawn to her anew. Plainly I was "stuck" on her as the other girls in the class were quick to observe. Later, when I was enamored with the image of Greta Garbo on the screen, I imagined that as a child she might have looked like Elsa. I was probably wrong, but what have right and wrong to do with infatuation?

One morning I was eavesdropping on what my new pupil was saying to the girl who sat across from her at one of the tables that served as desks in our improvised schoolroom. She was telling of her voyage home from Europe where she had spent the summer.

"There was nothing else open so we had to take the bridal suite," she laughed, or I should say smiled; she was not much given to laughter.

"The bridal suite!" exclaimed the girl, awed by the thought of such magnificence.

"Pooh!" said Elsa. "As if that was anything so special."

Another time I was showing my pupils a book of reproductions of Michaelangelo's paintings and drawings, among which was a detail of a group of cherubs, their vivid Italian faces crowned with mops of black curls. One of the girls (very fetching with her budding breasts curving against her brother's tight shirt she was wearing, and her long hair the color of old gold) studied the picture intently.

"Are those *angels?*" she exclaimed, surprised that heavenly creatures could look so dark, so Italian.

"Oh, no, Elisabeth," said Elsa. "Only blondes are angels."

Determined to be no angel, she would occasionally misbehave in class. This was obviously intentional, though I could not be sure if it was simply her way of escaping boredom or her wish to fix my attention on herself.

"Young lady," I said, putting on the sternest schoolmaster manner I could hide behind, "if you don't stop disrupting the class I'll have to send you home with a note to your father."

She did not seem particularly dismayed or contrite. Her old world eyes and secret smile told me plainly she saw through my weak facade. "If you do," she said calmly, "I'll tear it up before he sees it." She knew I had no intention of sending such a note, I had only kept her after hours to be alone with her.

According to Pascal, "the heart has its reasons the reason knows nothing of." But didn't Pascal characterize the state of man as "inconstancy, boredom, anxiety?" I wonder how many "reasons" of the heart may not stem from this familiar triad.

The last time I saw Elsa was on a beautiful day in early June two years later. Would it had been the last for then the memory might have endured outside of time instead of becoming only another way station on the road to oblivion.

My little class was no more; it had grown beyond the capacity of its amateur teacher. At my suggestion Elsa had stayed on for the few weeks that remained before she would be leaving for the summer, and after that for the New England school she would be attending in the fall to prepare herself for college.

I would miss her. I would miss her more than my conventional self dared admit. It was wrong, I told myself, it was absurd for a faithful husband (though if truth be told of one's self as readily as of others', faithful less by conviction than by convention) to be infatuated with a fourteen-year-old girl, a mere child. People don't do such things, as Ibsen's Dr. Brandt would say.

As I stood by the open window, waiting impatiently for my pupil, I could see my wife in the garden beyond the strawberry patch. Open book in hand, she had paused in her reading to bend over the perambulator in adoration of her baby. A tender picture, an idyllic scene; a devoted mother, a loving wife. By all the rules I should have been the happiest of men, but what I felt was my lack of feeling.

"Inconstancy, boredom, anxiety"—at twenty-seven I was the prey of all three. I had become a conventional husband.

I was about to turn away from the window when I caught sight of Elsa approaching through my neighbor's orchard. I remember how gloriously the apple trees were appareled for the rites of spring and how Elsa herself seemed to me one of their lovely troupe. How "slow and stately" she walked among them, a northern Primavera, her fair hair strewn with blossoms.

Fascinated, I watched her step from the shadows of the orchard into the fanfare of the sun, then cross the road and come up the garden path, pausing to wave her greeting to my wife.

We sat close together on the narrow bench in the kitchen dining room, each feigning interest in the text spread open before us on the table, and each with attention far removed. When we both at the same moment moved to turn the page and our hands met Elsa returned my gaze calmly, almost—or did I only imagine it—challengingly. I was the first to look away.

Abelard and Heloise, I though, withdrawing from the touch of her cool hand. Paolo and Francesca. I had read too much and lived too little for my years.

"That day we read no more in the book," I said, and closed the book and got up from the bench. Elsa too rose, with a sigh that might have been mine, and very much the proper young lady to my inhibited gentleman followed me out of the room and into the sunlight, and there in the doorway with a decorous handshake and veiled eyes we said goodbye.

Goodbye, Goodbye, love, forever. It is not so much our follies we live to regret as those we failed to commit when we might have.

Pity the man who dreams that, given the opportunity, he would not make the same "mistake" again. One afternoon years later—some fifteen years in fact—as I idled in my office, in New York, chewing the cud of the past, the phone rang. And when I answered, "This is Elsa," the voice said. It was the slow, low-register voice I had come to associate with Greta Garbo in her films, which by association led me to picture a mature Elsa in Garbo's beautiful image. "Remember me?"

"Elsa!" I cried. "Oh my darling? How could I ever not remember you? Where are you?"

She said she was living in the Village. I told her how absolutely delighted I was that she had called me. I must see her at once. We must have dinner together that very evening, I said.

As I came into the restaurant where we had agreed to meet, I did not at first recognize Elsa in the tall, rather lanky, not particularly striking woman who shook my hand. The years had left their mark on her (as of course they had not on me). Her golden hair had become brown and was gathered in a conventional bun. She was wearing a homely housedress that masked her figure, certainly no festive garment to resurrect an old love.

In short, I felt let down. I don't know what I expected. Or rather I do know. I expected to find a romantic image that had remained unchanged by time. At table I tried to hide my disappointment, and even—I could not deny it—my resentment behind a screen of small talk to which she listened politely, scarcely offering a word of her own. What a selfish, middle-aged spoiled child I was to feel the woman had failed me. And I considered myself a realist!

When we had dined I accompanied Elsa home. As we walked in silence through the soft summer night, I knew we must say goodbye for real this time, the dream was over. Yet when we reached the door of her house and she said, "Won't you come up," I followed her to her apartment.

It was a small place on the third floor rear with the living room serving as bedroom too. We sat on the bed and after a while I said, "Remember the last time we were together?" When she remained silent I continued: "You were so beautiful. I wanted to kiss you. I wanted to take you."

"Why didn't you?" Elsa said.

And so I kissed her now, posthumously one might say.

I was surprised, when she had shed the dress that had so offended my taste, to find she was what the French call false thin, with the well-formed body, the breasts, the hands, the feet of a healthy young Swedish peasant. She was all open to me, but there was no joy in my lovemaking. It was as if I wished to punish her for no longer being what she once had been for me.

Afterward as I lay beside her I felt sad, I felt guilty. I said I was sorry I had come too soon.

"Oh pooh!" she said, and got up from the bed and went into the bathroom. By the time she came back, I had put on my clothes and was ready to leave.

I never saw Elsa again. She called me several times at the office but I had told my secretary to say I was out of town. I can only hope she has forgiven my shabby behavior. I cannot forgive myself.

As I walked the sixty-five weary city blocks to my home that night I thought of Oscar Wilde's unhappy lines:

> So all men kill the thing they love,
> The brave man with a sword,
> The coward with a kiss.

Chapter 17

"Everyone," wrote Montaigne, "has a good curriculum in himself, provided he can spy closely enough into his own mind."

There are times in pursuing this memoir when I have to fortify myself with the master's encouraging thought against doubts about my own "good curriculum." What can it matter, I argue with my uneasy conscience, what can it possibly mean to anybody twenty years from now? (Twenty years! Say rather twenty minutes.) What I said to whom and when, or who said what to me, what I did or what happened on this occasion or that? Montaigne's proviso, of course, is everything. Without it an autobiography is apt to be mere gossip about oneself or one's past an exercise in egotism.

A man I used to know remarked one day in a mood of laceration about himself in particular and mankind in general, that early in his existence he looked in a mirror and it was the beginning of a lifelong romance.

"Maybe you should look again," I said. "Mirrors have changed since we were young." But he brushed aside my suggestion, said he was serious and I was only being facetious.

"Holy Moses!" he declared, taking off on one of his familiar flights of eloquence. "When I think of how many times, how many millions of times I have used the first person singular in my years on this planet; when I ponder the constant inane repetition of I, Me, My, Mine that will come to an end only, as the funeral people say, 'When death occurs'—as if death was some kind of accident; when I try to visualize the whole bag, subjective, objective, possessive, printed in the pages of a book, I see a volume as big and fat as the Manhattan telephone directory with nothing in it but I, Me, My, Mine."

"You have just added a few more," I said. "No use flagellating yourself. How could we talk, write, think feel, how could we be without our first person singular?"

With which words of wisdom I continue my nonfiction novel of the self.

I left Eden in the summer of 1928. I had had enough of the bucolic life. Restless, bored, I longed to get back to the city I had longed to get away from.

Before taking the train for New York with my wife and child, I picked up a copy of the Sunday *New York Times*. As I was thumbing through the book review section, I came upon a review of the then current O'Brien *Best Short Stories* and was astonished to find a story of mine mentioned by the critic as outstanding in the collection. I had not been informed by editor or publisher that Mr. O'Brien had taken the story for his anthology.

It seemed of a piece with the way the sketch had been accepted for its original publication. Remembering my days of discontent in the publicity department of the Edison Company, I had written it in what would seem to have been a moment of self-realization and titled it "The Jew." The next day I sent it off to Edmund Wilson who was then literary editor of the *New Republic*, though I didn't know Mr. Wilson and moreover was aware the magazine seldom if ever published fiction.

About a month later I heard from the *New Republic,* not in a letter of acceptance or rejection from Mr. Wilson but in the form of printer's proofs.

The little comedy which began so auspiciously with Mr. Wilson and continued so surprisingly with Mr. O'Brien was not yet played out. On my return to New York I had found a job in the public relations department of the Federation of Jewish Charities. One day, as I was scanning the latest issues of the Jewish-American press for evidence of my industry, I discovered the same story under the title, "A Gentile View of the Jew." How sweet seemed to me the uses of ambiguity. Just be glad, I thought, they haven't called you an anti-Semite.

My days as an "engineer of public consent" for the Federation were numbered. When the head of the department resigned to take another job, I had what I believe is called the "opportunity of a lifetime," that is, the change to jump into my predecessor's shoes at a considerable increase in salary. Characteristically I muffed it, for which I am not ungrateful. I thought I was supposed to promote the organization's annual fund-raising drive, but I found the problem was not as simple as all that. The problem was not how, it was who. The really important thing was to publicize the men who contributed time and money to organized charity; as good businessmen they naturally expected some return for their investment in altruism. Their expectations were modest; all they wanted was that their good works be recognized by their fellow men or at least their names mentioned in the newspapers. Thus: "Speaking for the men's clothing division of the Federation's annual fund-raising campaign, Amos Zilch, president of Zilch Clothiers, Inc., stated that . . ."

I should have heeded the cautionary tale my departing chief told me about his predecessor. The thoughtless fellow realized one day he had forgotten to name Mr. Zilch in the special story he had just sent by messenger to the *Times*. Grabbing his hat, he made a dash for the city editor's office to correct his mistake before the paper went to press. The editor was all sympathy. "I understand," he said. "We can't afford to neglect Mr. Zilch." And reaching into his circular file he retrieved the dispatch, carefully inserted the name of Amos Zilch, then threw the thing back into the wastebasket.

"So you see," said my departing leader, "you can never be too careful."

Actually I was not let go, though considering my benign neglect of my job I deserved to be. I quit first. Quit at the worst possible time, on the eve of the crash of 1929. After the second world war our superpatriots accused those of us who had come out against fascism in the thirties of having been "premature anti-fascists." I was now one of the premature unemployed.

Lewis Titterton, then an editor at Macmillan, had read several of my stories that had appeared in magazines. He suggested I tie them together in a "novel" he could recommend for publication. This I did by writing an opening section in which the principal characters came on stage and which I titled "All Talking" after the slogan then coming into use in movie advertisements for the new talkies.

I called the book *The Company,* sent the manuscript to Mr. Titterton, and was delighted to get a contract providing for an advance of $250 against royalties. It was a princely sum, none of your plebian six and even seven figure advances of today that have put mere scribblers in the same big league as professional baseball players.

The Company was published in 1930 when most people had more pressing concerns than somebody's first book. But the reviewers were kindly disposed, as they were for a piece I had written for a book of original essays published before the economic storm broke. (By "original," of course, I mean only that none of the essays had previously been published elsewhere.) I have long since forgotten the title of the book, though I remember the editor's name was Samuel Schmalhausen. I called the piece "All Dressed Up and Nowhere To Go," which was the way the twenties looked at me to the end of the decade.

Maybe I mention the favorable reception of my first book because I can't say the same thing for the second, *Between the Hammer and the Anvil*, published in the later thirties.

When I began work on this novel some years earlier I was what was then called a "fellow traveller." Presumably the term was invented by the communists to identify liberals and radicals who were neither card-carrying members of the party nor considered those who were sinister characters. You know, friendly types. Of the sort the wit must have been thinking when he said he could take care of his enemies, but protect me from my friends.

By the time the book was published, a number of fellow travellers had got off the train. They were now anticommunist, or anti-Stalinist—at any rate, definitely anti—which made them less kindly disposed than when *The Company* was published.

I was therefore surprised to find a letter from Maxwell Perkins of Scribner's in the morning mail. I had never met Mr. Perkins though I much admired him as the editor of Ernest Hemingway, Scott Fitzgerald, Thomas Wolfe, and other authors whose books meant something to me. When he wrote that he had read my novel and would I care to have lunch with him, I felt more than flattered. I felt airborne.

At lunch he asked me what I was writing those days and suggested, if I was not already committed for my next book, I might want to think of Scribner's as my publisher. I thanked him for his kindness, and he was kind indeed, but explained that not only did I not have a publisher, I had no book, certainly not in any shape to show him. This did not seem to bother him as much as it did me. He said if it was alright with me he would like to send me a contract. "But I don't even have a title," I protested. "Why stick your neck out for a maybe like me?"

Perkins was hard of hearing and I thought for a moment my remark had escaped him, but apparently it hadn't. "We'll call it 'untitled'," he said.

In those days an editor could do a thing like that; he could act on his own without having first to sell it to his boss the publisher. Today, when a publisher may be part of a company that in turn is part of a conglomerate, which includes among its various properties anything from a broadcasting network to plastics, the editorial question is no longer "is it a good book" but "will it sell"; the editor's eye is not so much on the book as on the bookkeeper. He may agree with Milton that "a good book is the precious life-blood of a master-spirit" but the question remains, does it tell the reader how to get his.

I am not talking about my own book. I was unable to write it to my satisfaction and it remains to this day not only "untitled" but one of those unwritten masterpieces. Shall I say life was too much with me, or offer some equally invalid excuse? How often I have heard some friend or other complain if only he had the time to write the book he had in mind, but unfortunately, and so forth. Yet perhaps fortunately, I want to say. If time were the only thing lacking . . .

When a year passed, and then another, and still a third, my obligation to Mr. Perkins began to weigh heavy on me. Perhaps it was only my way to avoid facing the obligation I felt I owed myself. I finally wrote Perkins asking him to cancel our contract, and enclosed a check in repayment of the advance he had sent me.

"What have you done?" he replied. "Whoever heard of an

author returning his advance? Now our bookkeeping department is in a tizzy. They tell me they had already written off the five hundred as a loss, and now they don't know how to apply your check. How could you be so inconsiderate? I'll do what you ask, regretfully, but contract or no I'm still interested."

It was a sweet letter and the thought of Max Perkins and his generosity to me remains green in my memory.

One day I received a letter from the Chase National Bank stating that the bank had a communication of interest to me and asking me to call at their downtown headquarters. I wondered what it could be all about. The only thing the bank had that could possibly be of interest to me was money, and I was not aware they were giving any of it away to penurious writers.

I was wrong. When I appeared the next day I was asked to identify myself. Had I any reason to expect a draught from a foreign country? I could only answer truthfully, no, I hadn't. Well then, my questioner asked, had I written a book called . . .

"Between the Hammer and the Anvil," I volunteered.

"That's it," he said, consulting a memo pad he drew from his pocket, and forthwith produced a check in the amount of $500. The check was courtesy of the Soviet Russian publishing organization, in partial payment of translation rights to my book. I don't know how it got to Russia; I had never seen the translation and wouldn't know how to read it if I had, but the check came in handy. I felt I had indeed "a friend at Chase," as the bank's advertisements said.

There would be no point in mentioning this incident if I failed to add that some fifteen years later, when I was summoned to appear as a witness before the McCarthy Committee, I was relieved not to be charged with having been a paid Soviet agent.

Chapter 18

But I'm getting ahead of myself. I should be back in the early days of the Great Depression. I recall Kyle Crichton's referring to those of us who wrote brief book reviews for *Scribner's* magazine as his ragged army. The admirable Crichton was an editor of that magazine while doing some of his best writing for the *New Masses* under the name of Robert Forsythe.

I was also reviewing for the evening paper, the New York *Sun*. My editor at the *Sun* didn't appreciate the popular bestsellers of the day, and he would save them for me to clobber on the Wednesday book page. Not that what I wrote made any noticeable dent in their sales, but I had the malicious pleasure of ridiculing the authors by quoting passages of their deathless prose. It got so, I heard, that publishers were reluctant to issue their blockbusters on a Wednesday to provide a field day for "that sonofabitch."

I met Ira Wolfert some years later, after he had won a Pulitzer Prize for his reporting on World War II in the Pacific. He remarked that, when he was still a student at Columbia, he could hardly wait to get out of class at noon on Wednesdays to see who my victim of the week might be.

"And now look at you," he said. "Sold out to the Book-of-the-Month Club." It was true I was then employed by the book club, but I hadn't thought I had sold out particularly. Subsequently I heard that Mr. Wolfert had "sold out" to the *Readers Digest*.

"When the whole world's giddy, one man can't reel." When the whole world's broke, one man can't be poor. In the depth of the Great Depression, when desperate men in New York were peddling apples at street corners and waiting in line for a free bowl of soup, my little family and I, including a Siamese cat, were summering at the shore. In retrospect it seems almost indecent. But we were not really shiftless, we were merely absurd.

The place was Rockport, at the tip of Cape Anne, north of Boston, where we found a cottage overlooking the beach. Not bad for people who were living in what might flatteringly be called straitened circumstances. Money was in short supply in Rockport that summer '32. Observing the number of paintings by local artists in the shop windows of the grocer and the butcher, I came to the conclusion that art was at last paying off; here was a new way to pay old bills. I could not help feeling it was the merchants who were getting the short end of the deal.

When November cold threatened us with eviction, we started back to New York, only to realize by the time we reached Boston, where we would have to change trains, we had not enough money to carry us very far beyond the Grand Central Station, which was certainly no place to spend the winter. Instead we stayed in Cambridge, in a snug little furnished apartment, until we were able to return to Rockport in the spring. Ideal, one might almost say idyllic. In these days of inflation it is astonishing to think how far nothing could carry one in those difficult times. As a matter of fact the general atmosphere in the Depression was more humane than it is now, freer, more creative, more hopeful. Or is it merely that we were younger then?

I am reminded of a story an artist friend told me of his own dark days. He was living in a back room on West Fourteenth Street when one day his neighbor in the next room informed the landlord he was moving to the house across the street. "What do you want to do that for?" his landlord protested. "You're not paying any rent here, so it can't be any cheaper there." "Oh, your house is okay," said the generous tenant, "but they've got a radio."

Even with a radio one still had to eat. The sea air of Rockport was bracing but it was not very filling. When I didn't know what to do for money, I would hop a bus for New York to pick up what editorial crumbs were left on the table. Among such I remember the manuscript of an alleged novel by a rich woman who wanted to be a writer. I was hired by a publisher to make her book seem readable, just as he, no doubt, had been hired by the author to make her book seem publishable.

What a bore! But I was more disturbed than I was bored by what I was doing—or rather not doing. I had been drifting too long toward no discernible goal.

Like the rest of mankind.

As if in response to my discontent I had a visitor from New York, a pleasant enough young man I had not met before. He said he was on his way to Maine, had heard I was living in Rockport, and had just stopped by to say hello. During our conversation he mentioned "they" had read my "things" in the *New Masses* and elsewhere and wondered if I might be interested in editing the magazine *Soviet Russia Today*.

When I asked him who "they" were, he smiled indulgently; he seemed to think I was pulling his leg. A leftist writer who didn't know the magazine was published by the Communist Party! After all, it was no secret; the publisher was named in the masthead. Only I had never read the sheet; as a matter of fact, I could not recall ever having seen it. Still, if the magazine's aim was what my visitor said it was, to tell readers the "truth" about what was still referred to as the "Russian experiment," it seemed to me a worthy enterprise.

Ah, the truth! The truth was my knowledge of Soviet Russia was as woefully limited as that of most Americans, my fund of misinformation and ignorance as unlimited. At the same time it seemed to me impossible to take as gospel the canards circulated by enemies of the socialist state in the name of anti-communism.

Will Rogers used to say "all I know is what I read in the papers." Today he might have added "and what I hear on the radio and see on television." And thus he would be able to sum up, for himself and for most of us in 1930, the "truth" about Soviet Russia.

"When ignorance is bliss 'tis folly to be wise." It was not until some twenty years later, when I read Isaac Deutscher's books on Trotsky and Stalin, and tried to think my way through the Russian maze with the author as my guide, that I came to appreciate the complexity of the situation.

Back there in the early thirties, I was much younger and therefore much more certain what the score was. Politically naive (again like most Americans) and a kindergarten student of history, I apparently thought it possible to be quite objective as editor of a propaganda magazine. (As if the mass-circulation magazines that littered our newsstands were not also propaganda vehicles for the established order.

However, if we're still talking about the "truth," let's admit that what chiefly appealed to me in the offer to edit *Soviet Russia Today* was the security of a weekly wage (thirty-five dollars). Also I felt flattered to be wanted for the job, flattered and intrigued by the idea of being a somebody and editor no less. In short, between vanity and need, egotism and idealism, I welcomed the invitation to come on board.

Given the nature of the assignment, it might be assumed I was a member of the Communist Party. As it happened, I wasn't more by chance, I would say, than by design. Nor was it ever suggested by any party leader or follower that I should be during my year as editor of the magazine, or later when I was book reviewer for the party newspaper, the *Daily Worker*.

Except by one "comrade," the friend and subsequent accuser of Alger Hiss—Whitaker Chambers. I hope to have more to say in a later chapter about this American version of a Dostoevsky character.

No doubt I was a simple Simon to think I was entirely free to edit *Soviet Russia Today* as I saw fit, without ever consulting the Ninth Floor (as party headquarters was referred to), or being told what to print and what not to print. This seems impossible in view of all I heard before and since about party discipline from the Central Committee on down the line, but it's a fact. It is also a fact that I had never set foot in the socialist state and could neither read nor write the Russian language. Perhaps Alexander Trachtenberg, the U.S. party's cultural commissar, provided the necessary link by attending our monthly editorial meetings.

"Trachty" must be dead long since—may the no-god of the atheists rest his soul—but he never gave me any instructions or caused me any trouble beyond my having to endure his nonstop harangues (with himself, presumably as audience since nobody else seemed to be listening).

It was during one of these instructive sessions I enjoyed a pleasant interlude making love on a desk top to the attractive wife of a colleague. I had gone into another room, ostensibly to look for some correspondence, and she had followed me there to help me find, I assumed, what I thought I was not looking for. When we returned refreshed to the meeting old "Trachty" was still orating.

I suppose it was not a very comradely thing I did, but then maybe it was. I came to think so several weeks later when the husband invited me to dinner in his apartment, which was somewhere to hell and gone at the other end of Brooklyn. After the dinner he insisted, as the hour was late, I stay the night—if I didn't mind sharing the only bed in the place with his wife, while he slept on a nearby couch. I was somewhat surprised but I thought it would be rude to refuse, even if it did seem to me that my host was overdoing the hospitality bit. I felt like a visiting Eskimo.

At the end of my year with the magazine, when I was still dreaming along in the comforting illusion that I was running an independent periodical, I found I was mistaken. It was my first encounter with the "party line" and it should have made a deeper impression on me than it did.

I was asked to a meeting attended by half a dozen men all of whom, with the exception of Trachtenberg, were unfamiliar to me, though from the discussion that ensued I gathered they were somebodies in the American communist hierarchy. It appeared they had recently returned from a world congress of party leaders in Moscow. One of the instructions they had brought home with them was that until further notice *Soviet Russia Today* was to be a "popular front" publication, and this called for a change of editors.

Popular frontism was the new party line. It was meant to broaden the base of acceptance by including nonparty elements in a friendly working relationship. But this is what I thought the magazine had been doing all along by inviting nonaligned American visitors to the Soviet Union to tell readers of their experiences, impressions, and opinions. Not to promote the party so much as to help bring about a better American understanding of the USSR and its people.

I asked those present at the meeting what kind of magazine did they think I had been editing, and why did they think the circulation had been growing. It didn't matter, they said. It was the new party line and that was that. Apparently I had been a premature popular frontist. Typically, the new editor appointed was an old party-liner.

I was witnessing history as it happens, not as it is written, or imagined, though I didn't realize it at the time. If today the Communist Party of the U.S.—whatever remains of it—is politically of no signifance, the reason may be that its leaders were not leaders but followers; they never learned to walk in their own shoes instead of Moscow's. Ironically it was Moscow's alliance with Washington in the second world war that put the American Communist Party out of the business.

When I say that my being fired from the magazine should have made a deeper impression on me than it did, I am remembering that my indignation did not prevent me from accepting the position of daily book reviewer on the *Worker*, which presumably was also to become a popular front publication. If anyone had questioned my judgement, I would probably have replied that the issues were more important than my pride. Vanity has a thousand faces.

If my questioner had then warned me that my connection with the communist press would some day cost me dearly—come the time of the witch hunters, the attorney general's list, and the congressional committees—I doubt if I would have listened to him. As editor of *Soviet Russia Today*, I had been accused of ignoring the fact that such repression existed in the USSR. Now I was being told it could happen here. Even if I had felt concerned I doubt if it would have deterred me from considering myself free, as an American citizen, to write as I chose and where I chose.

FDR assured us we had nothing to fear but fear itself. It sounded so fine and noble when he said it, but it was just another of those grandiose statements that mean very little in practice. The day was to come when I and a lot of others would experience "fear itself" and find it was far from being "nothing to fear."

Chapter 19

This chapter should be devoted to a chronicle of the literary left in the thirties, in which movement I played a small part. However, Daniel Aaron has researched the decade so thoroughly in his book, *Writers on the Left,* that there is no point in my attempting to cover briefly the same ground.

To the younger reader, as Aaron says, the events mentioned in his book may seem "as remote as the Peloponnesian War," while "to the veterans who actually participated in a few literary skirmishes . . . the story of their political and literary adventures between two world wars may seem unimportant, certainly not worth retelling in any great detail. 'Yet unto us,' as Cotton Mather said of some skirmishes of his own, 'it hath been considerable enough to make an history'."

Perusing *Writers on the Left* in my sixties, I could hardly be considered a younger reader, but to me, too, much of the ground covered in the book seemed as remote as the Peloponnesian War. Reminded of some of the things I wrote in the thirties, I wavered between admiration and embarrassment. I admired the conviction with which I espoused the revolutionary view, and was embarrassed to find myself such a pundit, so obnoxious a dogmatist. Not that I wished I could unsay any of the things I said then, though I disagreed with some of them now. What I regretted was that I could not exchange the doubts of sixty for the certainties of thirty.

Some time around 1937–38, I quit the *Worker.* I did not leave the paper because I saw it was "commie dominated," as Roy Cohn, counsel for Senator McCarthy's star chamber, intimated when I was summoned to appear as a witness almost twenty years later. Maybe Mr. Cohn was offering me an out as the innocent tool of the "communist conspiracy," but his suggestion seemed to me on a par with his question, "Didn't you know Earl Browder was a communist?"

It reminded me of the question I was asked by the proper authority when I registered to vote in Rockport. After stating my profession was "writer and editor," I was asked if I could read, and a page of printed matter was handed me to prove I could. At the time I thought the question rather amusing, but later it occurred to me my interrogator might have been a literary critic.

I left the *Daily Worker* because I was offered a considerably better paying position with the Book-of-the-Month Club. How strange, come to think of it, Mr. Cohn never asked me, "Didn't you know the Book-of-the-Month Club was capitalist dominated?"

One could actually change jobs like that in the thirties without being considered guilty by association and therefore undesirable. That was to come in the next decade when President Truman launched his "loyalty" program and his attorney general's list which led to the notorious blacklisting caper.

Shortly before my departure from the *Worker,* when America's involvement in another world war was still, as the Bible says of a cloud, no bigger than a man's hand—though it was by then a mighty big hand—I had a farewell exchange with the paper's chief editorial writer.

"Suppose," I ventured, "Hitler and Stalin should sign a nonagression pact."

"What!" he exclaimed, so explosively I was almost blown out of his office. "Hitler and Stalin! A nonagression pact! Are you crazy? Such a thing can never happen. Never!"

Too bad so many things that can never happen do.

To supplement my meager income, I had for several years been an outside reader for the book-of-the-Month Club, one of a number of first readers who reported on books submitted by publishers as possible selections. Then about 1937, I was asked to do some in-house work as well, and this eventually developed into a full-time job for me as the club's publicity manager.

The membership was growing rapidly and with it the volume of correspondence. This required the services of half a dozen young women plugging away at their typewriters to provide members with information to answer complaints and the like. My assignment was to review their letters and suggest possible improvements in "membership-relations."

All of which sounds pretty dull, and dull it was, but now and then I would come across a real gem that brightened my day. I recall one correspondent's reply to a member's request for the two-volume illustrated set of *Wuthering Heights and Jane Eyre* that the Club had been offering as a book dividend. Wrote the correspondent: "We would be delighted to send you *Wuthering Heights* but regret to inform you that *Jane Eyre* is completely exhausted.

Poor Jane! I could only hope she eventually recovered.

To prove myself no mere company hack but an astute businessman, I figured out that if the company could avoid using just one postage stamp per member/per year—in those primitive days first class postage cost only three cents—it could mean a yearly saving of some fifteen thousand dollars. Excited by the realization, I hurried to bring the glad tidings to Harry Scherman, president of the company, only to find him profoundly unimpressed.

"Not interested," he said abruptly.

"Not interested!" I exclaimed. "In a possible saving of fifteen thousand!"

"No," he said, probably irritated by my naiveté. "Don't annoy me."

I left his office quite crushed, wondering how what seemed to me a handsome sum that was considerably more than my salary for the year could so summarily be dismissed as nothing. I had not yet learned to think big in the business world. I never did learn.

However, I don't want to leave the impression that Harry Scherman was a rude man. On the contrary, I found him to be a gentle and considerate person, and the more I got to know him the more I liked him. One day I found him searching desperately for something on his desk. When I asked him what he was looking for he said, "my glasses." I pointed to the bridge of his nose where his spectacles were resting comfortably. "Oh, there they are," he said. "I knew I hadn't misplaced them."

To remind himself to bring some book or whatever to the office, he would mail a postcard to his home carefully addressed to Mr. Harry Scherman. What struck me as odd was the formality of his message to himself. "Dear Harry," he would write, "please remember to bring the following . . ." He could see nothing odd about it. "This way," he explained, "I make myself read the message because I think somebody else wrote it. Otherwise I might think it's only a memo I wrote myself."

He was never one to make excessive demands of his executives. I remember one time he was busy in his office writing an article for the *Saturday Evening Post* while his vice-president was negotiating the purchase of a ranch for himself in Arizona; his advertising manager was creating his own line of illustrated classics for some publisher; his direct mail manager was wintering in Nassau; and his publicity manager was busy with a radio interview program of his own—none of which activities had anything to do with the business that was paying our salaries."

"Then who's running the store," I asked Harry Abrams who was in charge of the club's advertising and who later became a publisher of art books.

Abrams, whose office was next to mine, pointed to the large room across the aisle from executive alley, where several hundred white collar workers, mostly women, were busily engaged with their machines.

"They are," he said.

After a few months as part-time assistant in the club's correspondence department, I had been given the job of publicity manager. I held this position for the next eleven years with some success according to *Variety*, which favored me with a piece about my "innovations" in book promotion.

One of these innovations I would rather not brag about. In my effort to keep the brand name, Book-of-the-Month Club, before as many people and as often as possible, I interested a major newspaper feature syndicate in serializing the current selection each month as a daily feature in the form of an illustrated digest, in plain words a comic strip. Think of how our literature would be enriched if we could "read" *Moby Dick* or *The Scarlet Letter* in comic strip form. I did my bit for masscult and am ashamed of my contribution.

Of the many conversations I had with authors on my radio show the one which attracted the most attention was with Gypsy Rose Lee (to judge from the way the curious gathered outside the studio window to catch a glimpse of the queen of burlesque).

Gypsy had written a book, though to look at her one might say it was hardly necessary; she was bright as she was beautiful. A born showwoman, she easily took the interview away from me, remaining center stage throughout the half-hour program. But what she said so politely on the air did not interest me as much as some of her remarks during a preliminary talk at lunch before the broadcast.

"Speaking of books," I said, "I understand you have read Karl Marx."

"Oh that!" said Gypsy. "I read his *Capital* thing when I was twelve."

"How extraordinary!" I could not help but exclaim, "I suppose you have lots of books at home."

"My, yes," she said. "You should see. I'm up to my ass in books."

In the course of our conversation, Gypsy mentioned that when she had seen Carl Van Doren recently at a literary cocktail party she reminded him they had met before.

"He seemed so surprised. 'Don't you remember,' I said. 'You were sitting third row center aisle and when I came down the runway I sat on your lap and ran my hand over your crew cut. Oh, look at the Fuller Brush man,' I said. He wears his wares on his head."

My conversations with Book-of-the-Month authors were of a somewhat loftier nature. One of these authors—by no means typical, I hasten to add—was a woman whose first book had hit the jackpot. It told how she had helped allied aviators, whose planes had been shot down by the Nazis, to escape to freedom. A book like that, published while the war was still on, was newsworthy. I thought it might be a good idea to invite reporters to interview the author.

As we were rehearsing her story, she and I, the day before

the scheduled meeting with the press, I happened to mention how thrilling it must have been for her to rescue all those aviators.

"My goodness, it certainly was," she said. "I could hardly wait to read the next chapter."

Happily there was still time to call off the reporters. Later I learned the book had originally been written as nonfiction, then rewritten as a novel, then rewritten as a "true" story once again, though not by the lady who could hardly wait to read the next chapter.

To go from the ridiculous if hardly to the sublime at least to the more serious, a privilege of my job was the opportunity to meet a number of Book-of-the-Month authors. One of these was Samuel Eliot Morrison whose *Admiral of the Ocean Sea* has been selected by the club's judges and who, as official historian of the U.S. Navy in World War II, bore the title of admiral.

It was at the time the charter for the United Nations was being formulated. The Harvard Club, where we were to have lunch, was colorful with the flags of all the war allies. Among these the Stars and Stripes was the centerpiece and was flanked on either side by the manners of Great Britain and the Soviet Union.

Pointing to the Soviet flag, Admiral Morrison said: "That won't be here long."

He obviously knew something I didn't know. It was only later, when I read Winston Churchill's "iron curtain" speech delivered in Fulton, Missouri, in March, 1946, that I realized the admiral was referring to the coming cold war which was in fact already under way while the flags were still warm.

At the time, I was more shocked by the tone of Morrison's remark than by the remark itself. So much, I thought, for the twenty millions dead in Russia, their homes, their villages and towns ruined, their fields ravaged by the Nazi hordes, so much for Stalingrad, the Red Army's—and the people's—prodigious feat in confounding the German war machine. But then, the admiral was a realist, an eminent historian, and I was only a sentimental fool.

Another luncheon guest I recall was John Steinbeck. He didn't think much of the men who were standing around the Harvard Club bar. "Ten percenters!" he said contemptuously.

"And what about you?" I said. "A fifteen percenter? I imagine that's about where your royalties begin."

Steinbeck may have thought my question as impertinent as I considered his remark. He didn't say anything.

Then there was John Marquand who, as we entered the dining room, riled me with his sarcastic "My, my, the Havard Club."

A Harvard man himself, the author of *The Late George Apley* was as much of a snob as the Brahmins he satirized.

"Sorry it's not the Somerset," I said. I was thinking of the story Peter de Vries told me about his visit to that exclusive club for proper Bostonians. He was in the company of his editor at Little, Brown, who was one of them.

"Why do these obviously younger members," Peter asked his host, "slurp around like pantouflards, dragging their newspapers along as if the daily news was too heavy to carry?" To which his host replied seriously, "They want to be taken for old members."

Marquand thawed considerably as our lunch progressed. He related his experience shortly after he had become a member of the Somerset. One day he was taking a piss, he noticed a wooden cubicle that looked like an old-fashioned, one-seater outhouse, and on the door a sign which said, "For emergency use only." He was still giggling about this while he was washing his hands when an elderly member at the next washstand asked: "What's so funny, young man?" "That," Marquand said, pointing to the sign on the indoor outhouse.

"I've been a member of this club for thirty-five years," his neighbor said stiffly, "and I have never yet seen anything funny about it."

Chapter 20

At monthly meetings, the Book-of-the-Month Club's judges were responsible for picking the lucky number in the raffle, which thereupon became the prestigious "Book-of-the-Month." After this, it was the custom for Meredith Wood, the company's vice-president, to phone the glad tidings to the publisher. I happened to be in Mr. Wood's office when he was talking to Cass Canfield, president of Harper.

"Yes, Cass," I heard him say. "I'm very happy about it, too. What? Oh no, Cass, not that one. We took the Richard Wright novel. You know, *Native Son* I think it's called."

The author was not only an unknown, he was also a radical, and not only that, he was even a Negro, and in 1940 the Civil Rights movement was still in its infancy. Moreover his book was a real shocker. That it would ever become a Book-of-the-Month and a bestseller must have seemed most unlikely to the publisher. Indeed, I wonder if the club's judges would have had the temerity to select the book if it hadn't had the well-established brand name of Harper behind it.

Harper had probably ordered a minimum first printing of a few thousand copies. Years later, when I was with publisher Little, Brown in Boston, the same kind of first printing was ordered for another striking first novel, Salinger's *Catcher in the Rye,* before it was selected by the book club.

As a then officer of Little, Brown had said to the editor responsible for acquiring the Salinger novel, "Who wants to read a book about an adolescent boy?" Subsequently the same question was raised by the same executive in reference to William March's *The Bad Seed:* "Who wants to read a book about a wayward little girl?" Only in this case the novel was rejected, to become another publisher's bestseller. The literary crystal ball gets a bit clouded.

But to return to Richard Wright. As we came into the dining room he, too, said "My, my, the Harvard Club," if from a different perspective than Marquand's. I could not help but notice that some members were observing us curiously and some not without hostility. It was only then I realized I was doing something that still wasn't done at that time; Whitey was not accustomed to seeing a black face in the sacred grove of his club. Other times, other ways. Today color is no barrier to membership; heavens above, even women are admitted. Man proposes but economy disposes; clubs need new revenue to remain solvent.

I asked Wright about his early reading, for though I knew his formal education had been rudimentary, he was one of the best read men I had ever met. He told me how, as a youth working for an optical company in Memphis, he had been befriended by a fellow employee who was a Catholic. "The fact that we were both members of minority groups hated in the South, he a 'Pope lover' and I a 'nigger,' made it possible for us to communicate."

"But he was white and I was black," Wright said. "He could use the public library and I was not allowed to enter, except when he gave me a note to the librarian so I could bring him some book or other he wanted. You know, 'Please give the nigger boy . . .'" et cetera. One day I plucked up enough courage to ask if I could use his library card. He didn't object but he wondered how I would manage. I said I would write the same kind of note he did and sign his name. The idea seemed to amuse him.

"I had seen a reference to H. L. Mencken in the Memphis *Commercial Appeal* and the way the paper denounced him for criticizing the South made me want to read his stuff. The trouble was I didn't know what books he had written, so when I forged the note I said, 'Dear Madam, Please let the nigger boy have some books by Mencken for me.'"

But I believe the author himself tells the story of his awakening in *Black Boy*.

Boy! 'Nigger boy'! It didn't matter how old a black man was, he was always "Boy" to the southern whites—unless he was a "Reverend."

"I was coming back from Mexico," Wright said, "and when we crossed the border into Texas I was worried. I was then a member of the party and I had a copy of Marx's *Capital* in my valise, not to mention pamphlets by Lenin and Stalin. A Negro communist who read books was certain to be an object of suspicion. Sure enough, when the customs man saw the literature in my luggage he gave me a second look.

"'What are you?' he asked. 'A minister or something?'"

"I'm a writer," I said.

"'Okay, Reverend,' he said. 'Take it away.'

"Then as I was walking off, I heard him call 'boy' and I froze. Uh, uh I thought, this is it. But when I looked over my shoulder I saw he didn't mean me, he was calling a black youth who was lounging against a post. 'Boy, help the Reverend with his bag,' he said."

Over coffee my guest was in an expansive mood. "I remember the time I was on a train in Alabama in the dead heat of an August night. Our segregated coach was oppressively hot and filthy. I was sitting in a front seat halfway between sleep and waking, when I looked up to see the perfect image of the traditional southern colonel standing there in the open doorway of our coach. He was so perfect he could have been something out of an advertisement for Kentucky fried chicken—white suit, black string tie, flowing white hair, elegant little beard—he was the works. He was observing me and my weary fellow travellers. His benevolent gaze took us all in and I heard him say softly 'the Nigra people,' as if he was blessing us from on high, 'the Nigra people,' visitors from another planet. Then he disappeared into his white-only air-conditioned parlor car. To this day I don't know if I actually saw him and heard him, or just dreamed him."

"Speaking of trains," Wright said, and he went on to tell a story which has always seemed to me a wonderful example of minority humor.

There was this young white liberal professor from the North who had been invited to lecture at a college in a remote southern town. When he arrived fairly late at night at the station where he would have to change trains for his destination, he learned that his train had already left and the next one was not due until eight the following morning. The professor felt chilled, tired and hungry, and he asked the man at the ticket window where the nearest hotel was.

"No hotel around here, mister," the man said "nearest one's about five miles away."

"But surely," the professor protested, "there must be some place nearer where I can put up for the night."

The man shrugged. "Only place I know of is down the street a bit but that's only for niggers. No place for a white man."

The liberal teacher from the North had no patience with this kind of ignorant talk, so he picked up his bag and headed for the "hotel," which turned out to be a shabby old rooming house. He banged on the door until it was opened and a black face peered out.

"What you want, mister?"

"I want a room for the night."

"Mister, we don't want no trouble with white folks," and the door was slammed in his face.

The professor didn't know what to do. Back again at the deserted station, he stood warming his hands over the oil lamp when he noticed they were getting black with soot. This gave him an idea. He smeared the soot over his face and neck, pulled his hat down and his coat collar up, and returned to the house.

"You all got a room for tonight?" he asked, and this time the door was opened for him and he was shown a room.

"Only one thing," he said. "Be sure to wake me at seven. I've got to make that eight o'clock train out."

Too exhausted to get undressed or to wash, he lay down on the bed as he was. The next thing he knew there was a hammering on the door.

"Past seven! Better hustle!"

The professor just about made it and, throwing his bag on the rack, he went to look for the dining car to get himself some breakfast. He had hardly sat down at a table when he was approached by an elderly Negro waiter.

"What you doing here?" the waiter asked.

The professor was surprised to be questioned, but he answered civilly, "I'd like some breakfast, please. May I see the menu?"

The waiter shook his head. "Dining car's only for white folks," he said.

"So?" said the professor.

"And so on get out of here. Don't make no trouble."

This was getting absurd. "But I am white," the professor declared.

"Don't mix with me," the water warned. "I'm telling you get out before they throws you out."

The professor was really angry now. "But I tell you I am white. Can't you see? Are you blind?"

And then suddenly it occurred to him that in his haste to catch the train he had forgotten to wash the soot from his face and hands. "Look," he said, unbuttoning his shirt to bear his chest. "You can see for yourself."

But his chest was as black as the waiter's face. "Oh my God!" he cried. "They must have waked the wrong man."

Wright's high crowing laughter when he finished his story made me think of the anti-Semitic jokes Jews seem to enjoy. A little laughter leavens the lump. Maybe . . . sometimes.

Black Boy ends with the future author bound for Chicago. His "Early Days in Chicago," which I published in the 1945 volume of *Cross Section*, carried the record further. The previous year, in the first volume of *Cross-Section*, I had published his novelette, *The Man Who Lived Underground.*

After he left our shores to live in France, I lost track of Richard Wright, though I continued to read whatever of his writings came to hand. Am I unfair to him in sensing, in books he wrote during his self-imposed exile, a falling off of his creative strength? I wonder if a "native son" can cut himself off from his roots, as Wright did, and not suffer a loss of identity.

I felt this particularly when I read the account of his visit to Africa. *Black Power,* published in 1954, still had much of the author's old writing strength, but it seemed to me weakened by his approach, which often was that of a knowledgeable tourist observing the natives. Wright even seemed unaware that the black glasses and colonial helmet he wore in Africa were hated reminders of the former white overlords. If I had not known the author of *Native Son* and *Black Boy*, and so much admired those early works, I might have thought his book was the record of a European's sojourn in the dark continent.

* * * * *

As I have mentioned *Cross Section*, a footnote is in order. *Cross Section* was the "annual collection of new American writing" that I originated and edited on my own in the forties, while I was with the Book-of-the-Month Club. It ran to four hardbound volumes published in as many years ('45, '46, '47, '48) and was reprinted in 1969. By "new" American writing, I meant simply that all the contents were "firsts," that is had not previously appeared elsewhere. A total of some seven thousand manuscripts were submitted for the four volumes, of which approximately a hundred and fifty were published.

Among the contents for the initial (1944) collection, in addition to Richard Wright's *The Man Who Lived Underground*, there was Arthur Miller's first play, *The Man Who Had All the Luck*, and Norman Mailer's early long story, "A Calculus at Heaven," a remarkable performance for one so young (but then Arthur Miller was only twenty-eight). Mailer had written his story in his senior year at Harvard, and it presaged his novel, *The Naked and the Dead*, an advance chapter of which appeared in a subsequent volume of *Cross-Section* (1948). There were also novelettes by Jane Bowles and Ira Wolfert in the first volume, a play by Paul Peters, stories by Edita Morris, Brendan Gill, Jay Williams, Shirley Jackson, Betty Baur, Nancy Wilson Ross, Lenore Marshall, and Ralph Ellison, to list only a few, and poems by Langston Hughes, Jean Garrigue, Edwin Honig, and Norman Rosten, among others.

Some reviewers raised critical eyebrows because I included the work of a number of well-known authors as well as beginners. Obviously there was no need for a venture like *Cross Section* if it was offering "names" whose work could just as well be published elsewhere. But also obvious was the fact that the work submitted hadn't been. Take *The Pismire Plan,* for instance, by the author of *The Friendly Persuasion.* Obviously Jessamyn West's 45,000-word satirical novel could have been published as a novel in itself. As a matter of fact it was, eventually, but not for some time after it had appeared in *Cross-Section.*

Chapter 21

One day shortly before noon—in, I think, 1947—Harry Scherman looked in on me at my office to ask if I was free to have lunch with him. I was, but I could not help wondering what the special occasion might be. He had never extended such an invitation before in all my years with the Book-of-the-Month Club. If now and then we did happen to be seated at the same table for lunch, it was always as members of a company group, presumably to talk business.

My curiosity was not unmixed with anxiety, though I tried to reassure myself that it was only the old reflex acting up, the ancient fear of the father. I have never been able to rid myself of that absurd what-have-I-done-now feeling when summoned by the boss, be he the great Jehovah or mere employer, nor to account for this deplorable trait in my makeup since my own father was the gentlest and kindest of men. Somewhere in my alleged mind is the idea, I suppose, of the all-suspicious, ever-prying eye of a punishing god who expects the worst of His children and is seldom disappointed.

Our usual haven for lunch on state occasions was the grill room of the old Ritz, which was then directly across Madison Avenue from our offices. My apprehension was therefore further aroused when Mr. Scherman, with his light, quick step, led the way to the more formal dining room on the second floor of the hotel.

As we sat down to table and pretended to be absorbed in the menu, I recalled having heard that in the old days, when he was discharging one of his women employees—before, that is, he became successful enough to have others do the dirty work—the boss would sometimes have an open box of chocolates on his desk to ease the blow.

Was today's unaccountable invitation to lunch to be my box of chocolates?

It was.

Obviously embarrassed, his eyes lowered, when we were having coffee Harry suddenly put down his cup, pushed back his chair, and abruptly announced, "We're going to have to make a change."

I had felt it coming but tried not to think what it might be. There was nothing in the record of my performance on the job, no word of dissatisfaction, to make me anticipate any sudden need to "make a change."

I felt hurt, bewildered, a victim. I think I also managed to smile—rather wanly, I suspect. What did he mean, "we have to make a change," and who was "we." Oh, I knew what he meant alright; he meant I was being let go. But why? I had been a member of the family in good standing for eleven years and the business was prospering. Then why?

It really wasn't all that much of a mystery, and there was no point in my protesting or asking for an explanation. Mr. Scherman understood that I understood, without his telling me, why I was being fired for no valid reason. He probably found the strained silence that had fallen between us as sad as I did.

"Of course," he was saying now, "we realize it's a hardship

for you. We'll continue paying your salary for the next six months."

I don't know how I found the courage to say firmly, "that won't be enough," for I am usually timid when it comes to making claims. Something must have told me I was being bribed to be a good boy and not ask embarrassing questions, so I might as well raise the ante.

"We'll make it a year then," Mr. Scherman said without a moment's hesitation. "Plus, of course, your bonus for the year."

And so it was I became another casualty of the cold war, a minor casualty but "mine own."

The previous year the Attorney General's List had been compiled as part of President Truman's "loyalty" program. Presumably intended as a screen for testing the political purity of federal employees, the List of so-called subversive organizations they may or may not have been associated with in any practical way "was a profound violation of civil rights in itself," as Gary Wills wrote in his introduction to Lillian Hellman's book, *Scoundrel Time*. It was "the basis of all kinds of later violations—by Congress, by individual employers, by entrepreneurial blacklisters."

The List, to continue to quote Mr. Wills, "was used to deny people employment in any responsible position, private or public. Any private citizen, armed with the List, could impugn another citizen's loyalty with what looked like the authorization of the United States government. From this single act arose the entire blacklisting campaign, the doctrine of "guilt by association."

As a former editor and writer for leftist publications, not to mention the communist "connection," I was plainly guilty beyond redemption and deserved to be cast into outer darkness.

Among Harry Scherman's friends and acquaintances there

were a number of ex-communists and ex-fellow travellers who were presently marching under the banner of anti-Stalinism. Now more red, white, and blue than the flag, they were bound to have advised him of my wicked past, which I had never kept hidden in any case. Under normal conditions—I suppose there are times when such may be said to exist—I think he would have shrugged off their warnings. But conditions were not normal; the Attorney General's List was not normal; the House Un-American Activities Committee—how appropriate the name—was not normal.

HUAC was having too much fun terrorizing Hollywood to bother with much else, but eventually it would have got around to book publishers and book clubs before Senator Joe McCarthy muscled in on the racket. In any case, among the million or so Book-of-the-Month Club subscribers, there was certain to be many self-appointed witch-hunters ready to denounce the company for harboring a Red and to cancel their membership in protest. Aided and abetted by the generally obliging press and electronic media, this could snowball into a loss of public confidence in the business and a considerable loss of revenue.

In short, there was no question but that in the prevailing climate Mr. Scherman had to get rid of me, however, reluctant he may have been to do it, and knowing him I like to believe he was reluctant.

My "resignation" caused no break in our friendship. Later, when I was working for Little, Brown, in Boston, and our paths happened to cross in New York, he would laugh—a bit self-consciously, it seemed to me—and he would point to me, as if to jest, "they can't keep a good man down."

Not much, I thought, not this time around. Next time they'll do better.

I don't want to make a mountain out of my personal

---

molehill, but of course I was worried about my livelihood as must have been many another victim then (and later in the reign of McCarthy), of the official "conspiracy" in the name of loyalty. With the Red-baiters riding high, my situation was not exactly favorable for finding new employment or a new salary comparable to the old.

Chapter 22

Looking back to my separation from what I had considered security, what interests me, what depresses me, is that, for all my "commie" theorizing in the thirties, how politically a neuter I was in the forties. Like Rip Van Winkle I must have been asleep for years. Now and then my slumber may have been disturbed by some nightmare of history, I may even have cried out in the moment's anguish, but I was as largely unconscious as the next sleeping man. Like any other self-satisfied citizen, I read bland references to the current lies and crimes, national and international, retail and wholesale, but was quite able to carry on as if everything was "normal."

This, even after I read much diluted reports of the Nazi systematic slaughter of German and other European Jews who were sold to the democratic republic for so many pieces of silver by their neighbor Christians. Also even after the suddenly silenced accounts of the Hiroshima holocaust "made in America."

Even after, even *while* manufacturing new and ever more deadly weapons of extermination in the name of defense, otherwise known as peace.

It took the shock of being separated from my job to jolt me awake. Only then did I realize how seriously I had erred by thinking the wrong thoughts, reading the wrong books, writing for the wrong press, associating with the wrong people—and what was worse, by not seeking absolution through public confession of my political sins.

I had actually been naive enough to believe that every American was free to think, to speak, to write according to his convictions, that indeed these "rights" were so "inalienable" they were not subject to question.

How absurd in an age of dictators! It must have been my liberal nineteenth century Harvard education that gave me such eighteenth century ideas. It had never occurred to me that some day in the mid-twentieth century I might be held accountable for believing in FDR's "four freedoms."

I mentioned this to one of my leftist friends, who had been prematurely pro-Soviet (before, that is, the United States and the USSR became war allies) and prematurely antifascist (before the United States entered the war against Germany) and was therefore triply suspect. He looked at me as if to say I must either be lying or be incredibly stupid.

I could plead guilty only to the second charge, which naturally I did not for a moment accept.

My friend sighed. "Where ignorance is bliss," he said, " 'tis folly to be wise." You're some Marxist!"

"Spoken like a true Marxist snob," I said, resenting his remark as one is inclined to do when criticized, especially when one feels the criticism to be just.

Yet in truth I never considered myself a Marxist or any other kind of "ist." I have an inborn resistance to hagiolatry. When anyone tells me that "according to Marx" one and one make two, or "as Marx said, "two minus two leaves zero," it sets my teeth on edge. I also have to confess that I find the master's magnum opus rather tedious reading, as trying as Kant's categorical imperative ("too German," as Charlemagne is said to have remarked when he rejected the ultimatum of a Teutonic chieftain).

Still, there were two great "Marxist" revolutions—the Russian and the Chinese—in my own lifetime. If, that is, one conveniently forgets it was in the two least industrialized countries that these revolutions occurred.

Ach so! Those iron laws of historical development! Who's to say that corporate capitalism, in its present phase of lawless multinationals, may not even now be unwittingly paving the way to a new order of international economy beyond the incentive of greed, when the great god Profit shall be no more and man's good dream of "from each according to his ability to each according to his need" comes closer to realization.

But that can never be, as my editor friend on the *Daily Worker* had assured me about another "impossible" maybe.

History, says Gibbon, is "little more than the register of the crimes, follies, and misfortunes of mankind." He was writing of "the triumph of barbarism and religion" in the twilight of Roman civilization. However, he could have been referring to our own corrupt times as well, in which case he might have substituted technology for religion.

What crime, for instance, in the entire history of mankind could exceed the wholesale massacre of the innocents in the Nazi gas chambers? Or that perpetrated by the United States when the infernal power of America's gift to humanity, the atom bomb, was tested at the cost of the lives of hundred of thousands of Japanese men, women, and children?

What folly could be greater—though lunacy is an apter word—what madness could be greater than that of our contemporary world, which by 1979 was squandering some five hundred billion dollars a year of the peoples' wealth to insure peace by preparing to annihilate itself?

What misfortune could be more lamentable than that of mass starvation? Yet with hundreds of millions already starving or seriously undernourished, mankind continues to increase and multiply. Meanwhile more than half of the world's available acres are being exploited not primarily to grow food for the hungry poor but to produce exports to further enrich the wealthy and the powerful.

I remember reading somewhere that at the height of the French revolution, when in one quarter of Paris the tumbrils were busy transporting victims from prison to guillotine, nobody in the next neighborhood was unduly disturbed, or even seemed to be aware of what was going on. In the years I am writing of, in Europe, in Asia, on the high seas, in Korea, in Vietnam, our young, friends and foes alike, were being mutilated and slaughtered, but on the home front all was quiet. Business continued as usual, in fact better than usual. War was apparently the health of the state. In any event the fighting and the dying were far from our shores, and it was not our country that was being ravaged. We the historically minded heirs of the ages, the proud defenders of human rights, considered ourselves safe and eminently sane.

I am reminded of what a bitter young friend, a veteran of the war in Vietnam, told me of his return home. He had hardly expected a hero's welcome, he said, but he was astonished by the indifference of his countrymen who talked and behaved as if no nightmare existed. "I was tempted," he said, "to reenlist so I might get back to reality, terrible as I knew it to be."

War or peace, four freedoms or blacklist, in retrospect it doesn't seem to have mattered which to Madison Avenue, the whore of our modern Babylon. I recall seeing an alluring four-color advertisement that appeared in the last year of World War II in several of our leading magazines. It offered readers the latest model in tanks! By the following year fashions had changed. Peace had broken out and tanks were passé. The new styles in automobiles had become the thing.

Like so many of my fellow citizens not directly involved in the "war effort"—(i.e., profiting from it), I had drifted through these criminal years largely undismayed by extermination camps and atomic blasts. Of the holocaust in Europe, we were told little or nothing at the time by our newspapers. I do vaguely recall reading that the emissaries of the Pope and the International Red Cross on investigation had found everything quite orderly, including, presumably, the extermination of millions of European Jews. Of the nuclear bombs dropped on Japan we were informed, after the fact, of their efficient performance in mass murder and total destruction, but not of their coefficient, lingering death by radiation.

The horror of the situation, of my personal situation, was that I had so little sense of horror. Death was in the air, but I had no difficulty breathing. Yet I think if for a single moment I could have experienced all the needless suffering brought by man to this earth of ours, I could not have survived the shock.

No fear of that. I was too well fortified by my "unexamined life."

Chapter 23

Socrates was of course speaking for himself when he said the unexamined life was not worth living just as Thoreau was when he wrote "the mass of men lead lives of quiet desperation." I doubt if the "mass of men" feel as desperate as all that, or consider their unexamined lives not worth living. One could just as well say the *examined* life was not worth living, it is so "sicklied o'er with the pale cast of thought" as to "lose the name of action."

But assuming for the moment that examination is all, if only it could come before, when presumably it might affect the nature of our acts, instead of after the die is cast. Perhaps it can, for a Socrates. But for most of us the act has first to be lived, life has to have happened to us, before it can be examined and its "worth" weighed.

I argue against my better knowledge that if I can see where I erred in the past (or where, presiding in the court of the present, judge I went wrong), I can avoid making the same mistake in the future.

When any man tells me he was a fool yesterday, he wants me to know that today he is wise. This is a dubious assumption on his part, as questionable as the notion that we learn from experience. Examining my own life, I see the anguish arises less from the recognition that I have behaved like an idiot than from the intimation that I shall go on being the same kind of idiot all my days.

True, we do manage to learn some things in the course of a lifetime, that fire is hot, for instance, and water wet, that the sun normally rises in the east and sets in the west; we can also learn some things about our fellow creatures and even about ourselves as viewed through our private windows. But it is doubtful if our essence suffers any sea change from experience, that we can ever become anything other than what we already are.

What I was at five I am at eighty. Examine my life as I may, the face I glimpse under the mask is the same face I was born ·ith

The longer I live the more impressed I am by what Freud termed the "suggestion" of his contemporary, George Groddeck "that the conduct through life of what we call our ego is essentially passive, and that, as he expresses it, we are 'lived' by unknown and uncontrollable forces."

That which lives us, Groddeck called our "It." Man proposes, and his "It" disposes. Life deals me the cards and my "It" plays my hand.

Small wonder that "man is born to trouble as the sparks fly upward." But also, how fortunate. Were it not for trouble, he might snore his life away to his last breath without ever catching a glimpse of himself as he is. He dreams of dwelling in the land of Cockaigne where cares are unknown, but he would not long be content there. He would somehow contrive to make trouble in its absence, even borrow trouble if need be.

A good husband I once knew protested that he was so happily married there was no reason for his ever being unfaithful to his wife. Yet he could not deny there were occasions when he unreasonably was unfaithful. Then not so much driven by remorse as by his need to suffer, he would confess on his knees before her, dissolving his sense of guilt in tears of contrition and promising what she neither asked for nor believed possible, to "sin" no more. I was not too surprised when she told me she had left him for another man who, if less honorable, was at least not as boring.

"Poor Formidable!" she sighed. "He could never escape the wedding ring."

"And who, if I may ask, was Formidable?"

"He was a diminutive Frenchman," she explained. "On his deathbed he begged his wife to grant him one last favor. All his life, he said, he had been plagued with the ridiculous name his parents had given him—Formidable—so would she please, please promise not to put it on his headstone. Instead she had these words engraved: 'Here lies my beloved husband who was ever faithful to me.' Unfortunately the burial plot was so near the sidewalk that passersby could read the inscription. 'Oh la la!' they said. 'C'est formidable!'"

According to Bertrand Russell, "the psychology of adultery has been falsified by conventional morals which assume, in monogamous countries, that attraction to one person cannot coexist with a serious affection for another. Everybody knows this is untrue."

I asked my friend which appealed to her more, an "attraction" to one man or a "serious affection" for another. She said she much preferred "a serious attraction."

I suspect that by "everybody" Russell had in mind the well-tempered Englishman who was so civilized he could make even adultery seem dull, and a crime of passion a breach of good manners. When he speaks of attraction here "coexisting" with a serious affection, there I wonder which is the wife and which the mistress; he might just as well be talking about interchangeable parts.

And then this business of "conventional morals in monogamous countries"; or in plain words the Christian idea of husband-wife relationship. In its unnatural war against nature Christianity has decreed that committing marriage calls for a mandatory life sentence without hope of pardon. Once two mortals are bound in "holy wedlock" they must forever faithful be "till death do us part," and so "With one chained friend, perhaps a jealous foe / The dreariest and longest journey go."

After travelling some twenty years on what we took for granted was the same road, my wife and I had come to a parting of the way. If the drama must have a villain I stand convicted: guilty as charged, of attraction to a number of women for more than one of whom I had a "serious affection." It is not my "affairs" I regret but their timing. They should have happened to me before marriage rather than after. What I learned would then have served me in good stead and my wife as well. They may not have made me a more lawful—or more awful—husband, but they might have made me a better mate for my woman and she a better woman for her man. Therein, not in the marriage vow, is faithfulness to be found.

That sacred vow, of course, is no more concerned with the individuals involved or their notions of faithfulness than is Mother Nature. Marriage is a social contract given teeth by organized religion. Therefore it is elementary that copulation in the marriage bed is not only lawful, it is righteous, whereas the same act perpetrated outside the marriage bed is fornication, a sin. But who needs a bed?

As Matthew the saint said, "Whoever looketh on a woman to lust after her hath committed adultery already in his heart." Any man still in possession of all his marbles and not altogether a hypocrite knows what Matthew said is true. Therefore any man who looks on a woman the way nature intended, if he would remain a good Christian should either castrate himself or gouge out his eyes. (The saint must have considered it unthinkable that a woman might look on a man to lust after him. I'm surprised that Women's Lib hasn't denounced him as a male chauvenist.)

Another saint, playing physician, advised "it is better to marry than to burn."

My doctor tells me Paul was giving it straight to the Corinthians when he spoke of a wife as a fire extinguisher. The trouble, he says, is that man, who is created in the image of God, seems to be the only animal continuously in rut. After the first several years of marriage, probably as little as two, his burning for the woman who happens to be his wife is considerably diminished. If indeed the fire is not already out.

The French, my doctor says, who are above all practical, have a better or at least a more sensible approach to the problem of marriage. To them, marriage means family. They apparently find it possible for husband and mistress, wife and lover to "coexist" without fracturing the family.

"At the end of the day the Frenchman goes to his mistress, the American to his bar. Which of the two would you say is more likely to be a faithful husband, less likely to resort to divorce?"

Chapter 24

And so midway on the road to oblivion—well past midway by biblical reckoning—the stumbling pilgrim found himself without a wife, without a home, without a livelihood.

Was my existence then as mindless as it seemed, and I no less the sport of chance than a bit of flotsam dependent on winds and tides for being cast up on shore or washed out to sea?

Idle question in whose rhetoric I seek to avoid facing the mirror I call my life. A human being is not a piece of flotsam, and what I call chance may in reality be choice, however masked choice may appear to be happenstance. What happens to me may be my own doing, and what I do is what I am.

No doubt there are those who can account for what they are to their own satisfaction, can balance their debits and credits as if life were a tidy bank statement, but I am an incompetent bookkeeper of my existence. When I review my days and my years they seem to me like the pages of my college notebooks. Each semester I would start a new one, resolved this time to keep a faithful record of what I learned, but the intention was always short-lived. At the term's end there were more blank pages than those filled with my scribbles, and these had become largely indecipherable. My path is littered with abandoned resolves and forgotten decisions.

I was quite certain I would never marry again, but then as Einstein said: "It's a contingent universe; nothing is certain."

Even in a contingent universe it was highly unlikely Helene and I would ever become intimate. Or for that matter our far apart paths would ever converge.

But they did, and we did, and who or what's to say it wasn't destined. If character is destiny, according to Heraclitus, then it must have been character that brought us together, I explained.

"Or maybe it was lack or character," Helene suggested. She liked to play the dumb blonde of the comic strips when I came on too intellectual for her taste. Her definition of an intellectual was "brains rinsed in cold water."

We had met in the late summer of '45, a few days after the angel of the atomic annunciation descended on Hiroshima, bringing tidings of a new age, irradiated.

Business of course was continuing as usual. It would take more than a nuclear holocaust to change our Madison Avenue way of life. Before leaving my office at the Book-of-the-Month Club for the day, I would check my desk calender to see where the nearest cocktail party might be. There was almost sure to be some publisher throwing a party in the neighborhood to promote his latest book and author. Who the honored guest might be didn't matter; it always seemed to be the same party anyway, attended by the same chattering busybodies in the same crowded room. But the drink was plentiful, and with luck one might find an attractive warm body who was only, let us say, semi-attached.

That was how I happened to meet Anne but for whom I might never have met Helene. She was sitting alone in a far corner of the room, nursing an Old Fashioned. When I said "you look lost" my subtle approach seemed to amuse her. "Right the first time," she said. She confided she really was lost, she didn't know what she was doing there, or who anybody was. "I must have come to the wrong party."

"You mean," I said, "you're not a member of the literati?"

"Literati! Sounds like some kind of Mafia."

I thought the lady was perspicacious.

In the course of another cocktail or so we became players in the comedy of mutual seduction. However, it was not until our third meeting that she yielded to my importunity. "After all," she said, "what else is there to do on a rainy afternoon?"

Anne, Mrs. Southey, (her husband was conveniently in Europe at the moment), was an entertaining companion, if somewhat given to didactics in the midst of more pressing concerns. Making love, she held at one such moment, was an art, or should be, not simply an acceptable rape. Otherwise sex could be such a bore, didn't I think.

(After Helene had risen some distance above my horizon, she confessed she had once asked Anne how I was in bed. "He's okay," her friend had reported. And then quickly added, "but nothing fancy," apparently much to the amusement of both ladies.)

One evening I had been participating in a radio panel discussion about a book I had edited. I was unaware that Anne was in the studio audience until the program was over and people were leaving. I suddenly caught sight of her in one of the back row seats in the hall. She was talking to a beautiful blonde who I thought must be the Helene she often mentioned. The two had met in Paris in the early thirties and through the years had become close friends.

165

Who can explain the nature of that violent attraction we call love at first sight, if indeed it be love. One actually recoils as from a physical blow.

"Was this the face that launched a thousand ships?"

Before Anne could introduce me I knew what it was to feel smitten.

But fair Helene only looked down her exquisite nose as indifferently she took my proferred hand. "Let's have a beer," she said dourly as the three of us left the building.

At table she changed her mind about the beer and ordered a martini instead. Anne and I had the same, but before Anne could lift the glass to her lips she spilled her drink. My infatuation with her friend must have been painfully obvious.

"Oh Anne!" Helene exclaimed in mock reproach, flashing me an amused glance from under her half-lowered lids as she pushed her chair back from the table. "Never mind, dear, there's always another."

"Ooh," she whispered to the waitress who had hurried to mop the spill. "I'm all moist."

The waitress blushed. I thought Helene was referring to the few drops that had dripped into her lap. "How naive can you be," she sighed when later I confessed I had been too far gone at the time to appreciate her allusion. Too infatuated with an imaginary nymph whose life in Paris of the thirties, as her friend depicted it, was so far removed from my prosaic existence.

Referring to her progenitors, Helene said it was too bad the Pilgrims had landed on the rock instead of the rock landing on the Pilgrims. La belle Helene, as Picasso referred to her, was certainly no Puritan.

"La belle indeed," Anne said, not without a trace of malice. "She was too belle for her own good. I tried to put some sense in her head, tell her she was throwing herself away on men who weren't worth her little finger. At least get one of them to marry you,' I said. 'You know men, certainly you ought to by now. Why should they bother to get involved if you're for free. You're not going to stay young and beautiful forever, you know.' I might as well have been talking to the wind. 'You're right,' she said, and went off to Brittany with a penniless artist who was painting her portrait. That girl hadn't an ounce of woman shrewdness in her—or a thought for the next day. Towards the end there was one man I think she genuinely cared for. But then the war came and she had to return to America."

Back in New York, Helene become the mistress of a wealthy Frenchman who was making the city his temporary headquarters. "I was his kept woman," she confessed early in our relationship. She still was.

I once asked a man I knew, and whose exterior was quite unimpressive, how he had ever come to be the husband of the loveliest model of the year. It was an impertinent question and the moment I asked it I wanted to apologize, but he only laughed. "You're not the first," he said. "I asked her the same question myself. I was the only man who offered to marry her, she said."

Not that I supposed Helene had any thought of marriage, not to me certainly, for though I soon grew fond of her beyond infatuation, I could not believe she felt the same way about me. I recall her declaring on one occasion, in the mock whining voice of a child crying for a candy, "I wanna be married," but I thought she was joking. I didn't realize how much of the little girl there was in the sophisticated woman. The same little girl who, on returning home after her first dance, had said to her young beau of the evening, "Do you really love me?" when he kissed her at parting.

Under the circumstances, I the husband of another woman and she the mistress of another man who could afford to "keep" her as I certainly could not, it seemed hardly possible, indeed hardly thinkable that Helene should ever come to "really" love me.

And so our idyll continued. Strange idyll of two opposites drawn together beyond their understanding.

Like any beautiful woman she could not believe what her mirror told her until she read confirmation in men's eyes. Sitting across from her at table in a restaurant, with one leg held firmly between both of hers, I watched her helpless as she indulged in that dance of the eyes which made me think of the gyrations of a moth around a flame.

"Must you flirt so outrageously," I reproved her.

"I wasn't flirting," she said contritely, "forgive me. It doesn't mean anything."

Not much. When I saw her again after a brief absence from the city, "why so sad?" I asked.

She sat beside me in silence for a long moment. Then, "I despise myself," she said quietly.

The night before she had gone to bed with another man. "I was surprised. I hadn't thought he even noticed me."

"I suppose you'll say it didn't mean anything," I said.

"That's just it. I didn't care for him in the least. When I wanted to go, he wouldn't let me take my things so I threw my coat over me—you know, the long one—and went home without them. I walked five blocks down Park Avenue naked as a jaybird under my fur coat and nobody so much as looked at me."

For a while she sat in silence again, in the way she had of holding her forefinger to her lips when she was thinking.

"I'm just a tramp," she said. "You shouldn't love me. I'm no good."

It was with much anxiety I viewed her imminent trip to Paris. Her boss, as she called the man who was keeping her, had

returned to Paris after the liberation and had ordered her presence. "I'll only be gone a few months," she said, but I did not feel
reassured. I dreaded her going. Though I remembered would she
forget? I was afraid I would lose her.

As it happened, her flight was delayed seven hours, and
we returned from the airport to spend the interval in her apartment where we had shared so many happy hours. It made our
parting doubly cruel.

"I don't want to go," she said suddenly. "Tell me not to
go. Please, darling, tell me not to go."

But I could not. I had not the means to provide for her.
Nor the courage to tell my wife the facts. I had only anguish.

I so looked forward to seeing Helene again in the autumn.
Instead there was a letter from Europe telling me what I feared
even before opening the envelope. She was going to marry a
Frenchman she had met recently.

Several years passed. I received another letter from Paris.
It was brief. "I don't know how to cross the shaky bridge between
us," the letter said. "I have left the fascist I was stupid enough to
marry when I didn't know what else I could do. I want to come
back to you. If I don't hear from you I'll know you never loved
me."

Chapter 25

To go back a bit, some months after I had "resigned" from the Book-of-the-Month Club, George Braziller reluctantly offered me a job working for his Book Find Club, he being too busy, as he implied, to attend to everything.

I say "reluctantly," remembering how averse his nature was to sharing any fringe of authority. Also remembering how long he kept me cooling my heels while he was making up his mind about the wisdom of his offer. At the time I thought his hesitation might be due to my questionable "loyalty" in terms of the blacklist. After all, we were still living in the age of McCarthy. I had been let go by one book club; for another one to employ an acknowledged leftist would be to invite the disapproval of the self-appointed guardians of the national virginity and a consequent loss of "members" (i.e., money). However, my fears were unfounded. Braziller was simply one of those who, not unlike myself, arrived at their decisions by indecision.

I had met him some years past when he came to my office at the Book-of-the-Month Club. He had just returned from military service in occupied Germany. He was a handsome, dark-haired, green-eyed young fellow whose well-fitting Eisenhower jacket and highly polished paratrooper boots, with the bottoms of his immaculately pressed pants tucked into them, made him look like a fashion plate of the elegantly attired G.I.

I knew he had started his Book Find Club on a shoestring in the thirties, offering good books, purchased from publishers' remainders, to subscribers at a bargain price. No reader himself, he had observed that the best books were seldom bestsellers, and were therefore available some months after publication at greatly reduced prices. The Book Find Club had originally been unmistakably leftist but was presently less, shall we say, sectarian in its selections and its subscribers.

Now he wanted to know if he could acquire for his outfit what copies remained of Anna Seghers' anti-Nazi novel, *The Seventh Cross,* which had been a fairly recent book-of-the-month. Very soon the judges selection of this "communist" book would have been unlikely, not to say unthinkable. By then the anti-Red virus in the United States would have been promoted too well by our alleged patriots.

When I explained to Braziller what he probably knew anyway, that no sale other than to members was permitted by contract with the publisher, we parted with a warm handshake and my expression of genuine regard for the kind of books he chose to distribute. It could not have occurred to either of us that before long I would be knocking at his door for employment.

Time flits by like a landscape viewed from the window of an express train. (Or why not like a plane breaking the sound barrier?) One morning I woke up behind a desk in the offices of the Book Find Club. We were having a very successful season. Selections which the larger book clubs had failed to make—like Norman Mailer's *The Naked and the Dead* and Tom Lea's *The Brave Bulls*—were bringing in customers faster than they could be served.

One day, on his return from a trip to Boston, Braziller

confided that while there he had talked about me to Arthur Thornhill and Stanley Salmen, president and vice-president respectively of the more than century old publishing house of Little, Brown.

In the course of their conversation, he said, he had advised them that what they needed was a man like me to take charge of their promotion.

Braziller was always a great one for advice given on the impulse of the moment and subject to change without notice. Why didn't I call on them, he suggested. It might be worth my while.

Which I did, and maybe it was, though when I first walked into the converted townhouse on the corner of Beacon and Joy streets that served as the publisher's headquarters, and saw the notice on the bulletin board adjacent to the old-fashioned elevator, I was tempted to run for my life. The message read: "Due to a malfunction of the operating mechanism the elevator is temporarily inoperative."

Shades of Emerson and Thoreau, of Harvard and the *Atlantic Monthly*! With English like that who needed a book?

When I met with the V.P., he naturally assumed I was there with Braziller's blessing, because I was interested in a position with Little, Brown. After describing the nature of the job, he told me what my salary would be if I agreed to come to Boston. It was more than I was making in New York but it was modest enough for the head of a department responsible for promoting a yearly list of more than a hundred new books, both Little, Brown's and those carrying the Atlantic Monthly Press imprint.

I was therefore somewhat shocked several years after I took the job when, in an intemperate moment at an intemperate lunch, Mr. Thornhill accused me of having "held us up" for the wages they were paying me. I had not considered myself a highwayman.

There will always be a Boston, I thought. Maybe it was time to think about quitting.

But here I am resigning from Little, Brown before I have even begun to work for them. Perhaps if we could read time correctly, we would be able to see the end in the beginning. Not, probably, that it would make any difference in the conduct of our lives. What is to be has been. I know full well that night must fall but I spend my days as if there was no night.

When I got back to New York and told Braziller I had accepted the position offered he was angry. Et tu, Brutus! He seemed to feel I had betrayed his trust, though in that case why he himself had more or less arranged for what happened was a mystery to me. But why try to understand another man's motives when we can't even understand our own? My friend reacted like the man who brings a companion home with him to admire his wife and then turns jealous when she seems to like the guest.

It was to be several years before my ambiguous friend and I were on speaking terms once more. Now, so many years later, if I try to explain that visit to Boston, or rather what happened to me then, I am stymied. It's like trying to recall the details of a dream one had a long, long time ago.

No dice. The past remains a sphinx. To console myself, I attribute my confusion at the time to Helene's return. If I wasn't so much in love and involved in a new marital relationship, I might not have done what I did . . . If . . . If. . . A life time ago I heard somebody say: "If I had an uncle would he like green cheese?"

What I regretted was not the radical ardor of my younger years but my present loss of convictions. It is true I had been a symphasizer. I had thought there must be a better way to run the store than boom or bust, war or unemployment. If I was deluded in this it was by nothing more suspicious or subversive than the belief that a saner world was possible.

I left the lawyer's office as heartsick as when I had entered. I felt there was something rotten, not in Denmark but in my own country, if a citizen had to seek refuge from unwarranted questioning by repudiating his past, had to submit without objection to the indignity of being "cleared" by a self-appointed group of his fellow citizens.

It seemed to me the real subversives who were undermining our country were people like McCarthy and his associates and promoters. In reality was not I, and every other citizen who failed to place the charge where it belonged, a silent partner to this subversion? I feared I would not have the courage to say so when I appeared as a witness, I would hide behind my need for personal survival, and therein lay the feeling of guilt I secretly harbored.

As I made my way home through Boston's "chartered streets" I thought of the cartoon I had seen long ago on the cover of an old issue of *Simplicismus*, the satirical magazine published in Germany before the advent of Hitler. There on the execution platform stood the condemned man, also his legally appointed mashed assassin, and three eminent witnesses in their correct frock coats and high silk toppers. One of these gentlemen was consoling the victim. "Just be glad," he was saying, "you were not a socialist."

Chapter 26

Huey Long is reputed to have said: "Sure we'll have fascism, only we'll call it antifascism." He should have said "only we'll call it anticommunism."

I was astonished, when I returned to Boston in 1949, to find the Cradle of Liberty so mired in McCarthyism, that bastard offspring of a U.S. president's "loyalty program" sired by a U.S. senator.

Not only could fascism happen here, it was already happening in the name of antifascism. The witch hunt was in full cry. Close as we still were to the Nazi nightmare it required no great stretch of the imagination to see its American counterpart present in embryo, and in the not too distant future an entire nation corrupted by the lies and lunacies of a home brew dictator aided and abetted by all right-thinking citizens.

As Richard Rovere says in his biography of Joe McCarthy, the junior senator from Wisconsin had no program; the Chairman of the Senate Permanent Sub-Committee on investigating was nothing more than a "political thug." But given another time, and another phony crisis like the "cold war," blown up out of all proportion by reactionary political-economic-military thugs, we might well see our Bill of Rights go down the drain of history.

If "eternal vigilance is the price of liberty" such vigilance was notable for its absence in the Boston newspapers and the electronic media. In the early fifties those eminent defenders of free speech and a free press had not only swallowed McCarthyism whole, they were promoting it in the name of patriotism. The century old New England publishing house of Little, Brown was itself under the absurd accusation of being a "red outfit," or at least "commie-oriented," and the local purveyors of news—like hounds that had picked up the scent—were in full pursuit, baying for blood.

Their attacks were focused on Angus Cameron, the editor-in-chief and a director of the company, whose independent spirit and integrity were well known in the American world of books. Inevitably some of the poison gas seeped under the doors of the house on the corner of Beacon and Joy streets, and some of the presumably reasonable men within were not so sure that the editor's politics were above suspicion. Wasn't he closely associated with the "commie-oriented" and even "commie-dominated" bunch, the Progressive Party?

If he had wanted to compromise, that is to talk out of both sides of his mouth, he could probably have weathered the storm. Arthur Thornhill, president of the company, was a hard-headed, old-style Yankee conservative who was not easily persuaded that he might be mistaken, and Cameron was his man. When the push came to shove he would most likely have stood by his editor. But Cameron was fed up with the hypocrisy of some of his fellow directors. He could have accepted, however reluctantly, their rejection of a new novel by an alleged leftist author whose previous books they had published without dissent, also with some profit to the company. What he could not accept was their basing their present rejection on aesthetic grounds. They had suddenly become literary critics.

Cameron was out of the state visiting one of his authors when he received a peremptory message from headquarters demanding that henceforth he cease and desist from any "outside"—read "political"—activities without the consent of his fellow directors.

When I came into his office the day he resigned I found him clearing his desk. It was a melancholy scene, although he was his usual cheerful self. I thought of the framed motto in the office of one of our associates. It was in Latin and I, a poor Latinist, thinking it might be a quotation from Virgil or some other noble Roman, had asked the occupant to translate it for me. "It says," he explained, "Don't let the bastards get you down."

Howard Cady, who succeeded Cameron as Little, Brown's chief editor, told me he too had a motto he would like to have framed for his office but he was not sure how the Latin should read. Translated loosely the motto said, "It's difficult to shit on a moving target."

With Cameron out I was bound to be the next logical target of the patrioteers. My political coloring was alleged to be more pronounced red than Cameron's and my position at Little, Brown was nowhere near as important to the company as his; I could be let go with far less concern, if any, on the part of the management. When I read the mealy-mouthed letter the company sent to booksellers, absolving the publisher from any taint of heresy, I felt like letting myself go, but as I had nowhere to go but down and out I ruled against my better self.

Shortly thereafter I received an invitation to appear as a witness before the McCarthy Committee.

The defenders of our national innocence must have been scraping the bottom of the barrel when they subpoenaed anybody as unimportant for their purposes as I was. I had thought my commie past was buried under some twenty years of indifference, not to mention unawareness that I even existed. But murder, as they say, will out.

It was like a recurrent anxiety dream I used to have, that evidence of a crime I had committed so long ago I had completely forgotten about, had been uncovered. How could I ever have been so careless as to forget, or to assume the law would not remember? Now the bones had been unearthed, the murder revealed, the criminal indicated. My guilt was plain for all to see; there was no place for me to hide. Soon the police, maybe tomorrow, maybe even now would be knocking at my door.

Oh, how could I ever! How could I ever . . . ? At which point of anguish I would wake up, in a cold sweat but immensely relieved it was only a dream, that after all I was—well, innocent of course, a comforting self-deception.

But the summons handed to me in my office at Little, Brown by a seedy messenger of the gods was no dream, and I read it with growing dismay. I was frightened. A public hearing with all its attendant publicity could very well cost me my job. Not that I had any illusion I was big news; very little, or none, would do. Word from Washington would get back to Boston before I did, and when I arrived I would find the axe waiting for the victim.

I could ill afford to be fired. With no savings and two bank loans, however small, also with several people depending on my pay check, I wouldn't know where to turn. Once the witch's mark was on me, finding a position with another publisher, or for that matter finding any job would be difficult if not impossible in the prevailing climate of fear. Only those who have survived that orgy of national insanity can appreciate the virulence of the disease spread by Senator McCarthy and his fellow conspirators in Congress anɑ elsewhere, with the assistance of such hucksters of panic as *Aware, Inc.* and *Red Channels,* the guide for the complete witch hunter. I had seen how better, more talented men than myself had been hounded for refusing to cooperate with their persecutors, their careers, their very lives wrecked by evil innuendo.

It was therefore with some fear and trembling I saw a lawyer before leaving for Washington. He was one of the company's attorneys Mr. Thornhill had kindly suggested I might want to consult.

I told the lawyer that because I had written for the American Communist Party press in the early thirties I was afraid "they" wouldn't believe me when I said I had not been a party member.

"Well," he said, leaning back in his chair as he puffed contentedly at his pipe, "you can hardly fault them for that."

I resented his saying this, particularly as I agreed with him. At the same time I felt I would be faulting myself if I consented to be questioned about my politics which seemed to me strictly my own business as an American citizen.

"Why did you?" he said. "I mean why did you work for them?"

"I needed to eat. Jobs were scarce in those days and I took the first one offered me. It never occured to me that I was doing anything questionable, let alone that I would be called to account for it twenty years later."

"Then tell them so. You've got nothing to worry about."

Not much, I thought. Would my advisor be so much at ease if he were in my shoes?

"Anyway, they've got the answers before they ask the questions. The record will show if you're telling the truth." He struck a match to his pipe. "Still, you must have been a sym-

SO FAR SO GOOD

pathizer, a fellow traveller as they call it. I mean after all . . ."

It was an interesting point. I mean after all, if I had worked for a Hearst paper, or a Scripps-Howard, if I had been connected with the capitalist press in any capacity, nobody would ever think of accusing me of having been a Republican or a Democrat or a fellow-traveller of one of these political parties.

Chapter 27

The subpoena said I was to materialize in a certain room in Washington at a specific hour, but when I arrived I found nobody home. After a while a secretary wandered in, asked me for my name and address, then wandered out, leaving me to continue sitting alone in the empty room. Eventually a sleek, clever-looking young man appeared. I had seen his picture in the newspapers enough times to recognize it was Roy Cohn, counsel for McCarthy's band of senatorial vigilantes.

Mr. Cohn jerked his head toward a far corner of the room indicating that I was to join him there in some sort of secret conference. I couldn't see any need for secrecy since there was no one else present.

"Are you a fifth amendment case?" he asked abruptly.

"What's that?" I said I didn't understand, which happened to be true. There are occasions when I am more than normally obtuse and this was one of them.

"Oh, you know," Mr. Cohn said with an impatient jerk of his shoulders. "Are you going to plead the fifth amendment?"

"I hadn't intended to," I said. "Why? Should I?"

"You mean you're going to deny you're a communist!" Mr. Cohn sounded scandalized.

I felt my temperature rising. "What do you want me to do, perjure myself? If I say I'm not a member of the Communist Party, I'm not.

This of course was not what he had asked me. How neatly I had accommodated him, however, not only by seeming to equate the idea of communism with membership in the party, which was his familiar play, but also to repudiate both when there was nothing illegal in either.

I recalled the demonstration I had witnessed in the thirties in front of New York's city hall. The crowd was demanding bread and jobs and the police were offering clubs. In the midst of the fracas one man cried out to a copy who was bearing down on him: "But I'm an *anti*-communist!" "I don't care what kind of goddamned communist you are," the officer declared as he applied his club to the poor fellow's head.

Mr. Cohn couldn't care less what kind of communist I was. In fact he suddenly became affable, even confiding. "The senator can't make it this afternoon," he said. "He has to be on the floor for the Bohlen case." I gathered the great man was busy contesting the appointment of Mr. Bohlen as ambassador to the Soviet Union. "Senator Jackson will be taking his place. He should be along shortly."

The gentleman from the sovereign state of Washington having duly arrived, we got down to business and Mr. Cohn began his familiar litany. "Are you now or have you ever been a member of? . . ." It occurred to me that by this late date, instead of counting sheep at night my interrogator must lull himself to sleep with these words. He certainly seemed to be lulling Senator Jackson.

"Have you ever associated with any known communists? asked Mr. Cohn.

"I suppose I must have associated with some," I said,

"without knowing what their party affiliation was, and known others without being what you call associated with them."

"Who, for instance."

"Well, let's say Earl Browder. I knew him slightly but I can't say I associated with him."

"Didn't you know he was a communist?"

"How could I not know? It was no secret he was his party's candidate for president. The *New York Times* said so in a front page story."

"Humph!" grunted Mr. Cohn.

I didn't know what he was leading up to but I had a feeling he might be fishing for names. My only real worry, aside from the fear of losing my job, was that I might be asked to identify this person or that as a "known" communist. Several men and women I knew, or knew of, who in normal times would never think of themselves as informers, had become "cooperative witnesses." I had no wish to be included in their company.

"Did you ever attend any communist meetings?" Mr. Cohn was asking now.

"You mean party meetings. I don't know, I guess you could call them party meetings if you wanted to. I remember one that was called by the management of the *Daily Worker* and all staffers were asked to attend."

Mr. Cohn wanted to know what happened then.

"Nothing much. The purpose, as I remember it, was to discuss what we could learn from the capitalist press about running a newspaper. God knows, they had plenty to learn; I say 'they' because I had nothing to do with management. The meeting had hardly got under way before it was bogged down in philosophical arguments, ideological questions, that sort of thing. Before it ended they were discussing the Talmud. I never have understood how the Talmud got into the act."

Mr. Cohn was not amused, "Any other meetings?" he asked.

"Yes, come to think of it, there was another one. That was even worse. I didn't know anybody there. I certainly didn't know why I was there. They were talking about union politics, boring from within or something like that. Anyway, it sure was boring."

"And what did you do?"

"Me? I didn't do anything. I left as soon as I decently could."

"Why? Because you saw it was commie dominated?"

Commie dominated! that idiot phrase, repeated yet once again, made my flesh creep.

"No," I said, "I left because I was bored. I was bored from within and from without."

"I see," said Mr. Cohn.

What did he see, I wondered as one dreary question followed another. The thought that even for a moment I could lead him to believe I was a "cooperative witness" made me angry. Who gave him the right to question me like a prisoner in the dock? Weren't we supposed to be equal citizens in the eyes of the law? Even a criminal was entitled to be told the crime he was charged with. I felt like the character in Kafka's novel, *The Trial*.

Suddenly Senator Jackson who had been sleeping, it seemed to me, with his eyes open, shook himself awake.

"Would you say then," he asked, "that you didn't have any further affiliation after the Russian-Finnish war?"

I didn't bother to ask him what he meant by "affiliation." It seemed that for the senator the war had been some kind of watershed. If you were a Red before the conflict, you might have been mistaken or misbegotten, maybe even misforgiven. But after the war was over and you still continued to be a political heretic, Heaven forbid!

Chapter 28

The question and answer period was over. The senator left the room and I, too, was about to leave when Mr. Cohn detained me.

"You've been very cooperative," he said. "We'll want you to appear at the public hearing tomorrow."

Here we go, I thought. "You mean television and all that sort of thing?" I said, plainly dismayed.

"It won't be so bad," Mr. Cohn said. "You'll see. It'll only take a few minutes." It sounded like the encouraging remarks of a dentist before he yanks a sore tooth out of your mouth. Or maybe the consoling words of the executioner's assistant as he straps the condemned to the chair and fixes the electrodes.

My good angel came to my aid. Maybe my good angel is just ordinary shrewdness; I have been accused of that, too. Anyway, something told me Mr. Cohn was the kind of man who likes to make a deal and, though I was in no position to bargain, I said: "Look, I'll do as you say if you'll do something for me."

"What's that?" he said. He seemed suspicious.

"I'm here on my own. Right? But I happen to work for a publisher in Boston, as you know, and I need my job. If you bring up my association with the company I'm a dead duck. So I ask you please not to mention the name of Little, Brown.

This time Mr. Cohn really surprised me. "I can't promise," he said considerately, "but I'll speak to the senator about it."

The last thing I expected the next day when I took the stand in the crowded chamber (with Senator McCarthy seated in the center of his fellow inquisitors at the long table on the dais in a kind of travesty of da Vinci's *The Last Supper*)—the last thing I could possibly have anticipated was to see the senator hold high a copy of my first book, *The Company.*

"Did you write this book?" he asked.

I pleaded guilty though I didn't know what of. Surely my inoffensive little book couldn't be that bad.

The Company had been published by MacMillan more than twenty years before and was long out of print. In fact, I did not own a copy myself; someone had borrowed mine and failed to return it. Now when the senator like an auctioneer displayed the book for all to see, I wanted to raise my hand and make a bid for it. In any event, it was completely innocent of any political content whatsoever and could not be considered subversive by any stretch of the official imagination or lack thereof. It was unlikely that either lawyer Cohn or his senator boss had ever read a single page. Since the author was a "known communist," his book must be communist too. They didn't have to read it to know that.

Possibly those "junketeering gumshoes," Mr. Cohn and his friend Mr. Schine, had found *The Company* in one of the American libraries during their sojourn in Europe presumably to ferret out home-grown Reds. By that time, writes Richard Rovere, "most of the 'offending' books had been thoroughly bowdlerized by the State Department." It seemed the committee had never heard of my second novel which they might well have considered to be "commie oriented." The anti-Stalinist reviewers had done such a good job of burying *Between the Hammer and the Anvil* the corpse could not be disinterred.

I have always regretted that when Mr. Cohn posed the question: "If you were trying to do what we're trying to do, would you have your book in an American library abroad?" I did not have the common sense to reply the way it was said Dashiell Hammett did when he was asked the same question.

"If I were trying to do what you're trying to do," Hammett said, "I wouldn't have any book in any library."

Instead I answered the question not without strict logic but without sincerity, "No." I knew Mr. Cohn was fishing again and I didn't want to be hooked. All I wanted was to make my getaway without mention of Little, Brown, or any other names. I consoled myself with the thought that I wasn't implicating anyone, I wasn't betraying anyone, I wasn't harming anybody but myself, and I could live with that.

But inwardly I couldn't. I felt humiliated, and when I reviewed the situation I knew my reasoning was specious. I had answered Mr. Cohn's question not out of conviction (that much, I hoped was obvious) but out of concern for my own welfare, on which several people besides myself were dependent.

It was only years later I learned that some I considered to be my friends at the time, among whom were several self-styled revolutionaries who had sacrificed nothing for the "cause" or been deprived of a livelihood for their views, had accused me of being a "cooperative witness" who had "repudiated" his own book. I said such talk was nonsense, that if they had read the book they must have seen there was nothing to repudiate. But no matter how much I rejected the imputation of my holier-than-thou friends, or how small I chose to think my fault was, I felt the fault was there, that it has been motivated by ignoble fear, and I have suffered in the recognition of this.

After a few more questions of the same sort as I had answered the day before, the hearing was over and I was dismissed. I was safe. I was "cleared."

It was with an unhappy conscience that I took the first train back to Boston.

Chapter 29

When I came into the dining car, the nearest seat available was at a table already occupied by two men and a woman. They seemed to be travelling together, also to be somewhat inebriated. They were sales people, I gathered from their conversation, going to or returning from a convention. Somehow in the course of their meandering exchange they got to talking with considerable hilarity about lemmings—a species of animal or rodent, they were not sure which—of whose habits they were obviously less than adequately informed.

In the midst of their discussion came a voice from across the aisle explaining precisely what lemmings were and why they behaved as they did. Curious, I looked to see who was instructing my table companions. Our eyes met, and I was about to exclaim as I live and breathe it's Whittaker Chambers when he cut short his dissertation, grabbed his hat from the rack and hurriedly left the car.

I wondered why the rush. At the same time I did not wonder. Old Whit always was a man of mystery. If the mystery did not exist, he would manage to create it. Presently, he was Time Inc.'s and Washington's anticommunist authority, renegade par excellence and betrayer of confidences he had either invited and nourished or planted himself for future plucking. He was a busy fellow.

I had first met Chambers back in 1931 when he was, for a brief interval, editor of the *New Masses*. An avowed communist he was then. He was as Daniel Aaron says in *Writers on the Left*, "a literary proletarian luminary" after the publication of his story, "You Can Make Out Their Voices." (The story was subsequently published as a pamphlet under the title "Can You Hear Their Voices" and produced as a play at Vassar College by Hallie Flanagan.) I had written several sketches and critical articles for the *New Masses* before he became editor and was calling on him now at his office by invitation.

Lolling back in his chair with his hands clasped on top of his head, Chambers was smiling affably, very friendly, indeed avuncular, although we were both about the same age.

"It's not enough to be a liberal, or even a leftist, writer," he admonished me softly. "You should be a party writer."

I mention he spoke softly for want of a better word to describe how his voice struck me at the moment, but a few minutes later, when he answered the telephone, "conspiratorially" seemed more precise. Although he was sitting no more than two or three feet away from me, in fact just the other side of the desk, I could not make out a thing he was saying; his voice seemed to be swallowed by the mouthpiece of the phone. I left his office more impressed by this than by his suggestion I become a card-carrying "party writer," which translated itself in my mind as party hack.

I did not see Chambers again until the following year; after editing only a few issues of the magazine, he had simply dropped out of sight. I remember it was on a dark rainy evening at the height, or should I say depth, of the great Depression, as indeed was I. The sudden heavy downpour that had caught me quite unprepared on the way to the apartment of Maxim Lieber, my then literary agent, didn't help any. Lacking raincoat or umbrella, I was pretty well drenched by the time I rang the bell.

I had no idea Lieber also represented Chambers, or even knew him, but there to my surprise was Whittaker in the flesh with his blubber body sprawled on a couch. From the moment of awkward silence that followed my appearance, I got the impression that they had been talking about something I was not supposed to hear. But this may be only a later notion of mine, part of the general suspicion I came to have for everything connected with Chambers.

When the time came to say goodbye, he proposed I accompany him home and spend the night at his place. As I had nothing else to do and no money to do it with I accepted his invitation, which I never would have done had I known his destination—Weehawken, of all places. At least I thought that's where the ferry across the Hudson was depositing us that gloomy rain-soaked night. From there we proceded, by deserted bus, to some dark street somewhere and disembarked to climb a flight of outside steps to an apartment.

Weary and dispirited as I felt, I found some comfort in the well-lighted warmth and bourgeois comfort of the place. After the double shot of rye my host poured each of us, I was able to lift my head and look around, if somewhat dizzily as I had eaten nothing since breakfast.

What I saw on the wall to my left was a big poster-size photograph of Franklin Delano Roosevelt. And facing the president, on the wall opposite, an equally large poster-size picture of Adolph Hitler, swastika and all.

"Hey, Whit," I said, "what's the idea?"

"The idea of what?" he said.

I pointed to the poster of Hitler.

"Oh that!" he said, dismissing the fuehrer with a wave of his hand. "Window dressing!"

"I never know who might be paying me a visit when I'm not here."

"You mean . . . ?"

"Sure. Going through my papers. You know."

I didn't know but I let it go at that. Nobody had ever taken the trouble to look through *my* papers. This fellow Chambers was a character, no doubt about it.

"What are you doing these days?" I asked.

"Haven't decided," he said. "I may take some chemistry at Columbia. Or I may have to leave for Russia. You know . . ."

Again I didn't know, but it seemed to me things were growing more mysterious by the minute. "Why chemistry?" I said.

"There's a war coming. A knowledge of chemistry will be important."

War, chemistry, Russia, window dressing . . . I felt lost somewhere in a spy novel. At the same time I wasn't sure Chambers might not be pulling my leg. It was all too opera bouffaish for me.

As I drifted off to sleep I wondered if the whiskey had gone to my head. But then that picture of Hitler . . .

The next morning the picture was still there and it was still raining hard.

"Look, Whit," I said, as we waited at the corner for the bus to take us back to the ferry, "what were you saying last night about maybe having to go to Russia?"

"Shhh," he said, looking around him apprehensively. "Not so loud."

I too looked around. The street was absolutely, depressingly deserted. Not a soul to be seen anywhere.

"You never know who might be listening," he said.

What with one thing and another I thought of Pyotor Verkhovenski in *The Possessed* and Nechayev, the real if incredible original of Dostoevsky's archconspirator. If Chambers was a natural as Judas he was also a born fantasist. When he eventually confessed to having been a communist agent—which was presumably alright by then because he was now cooperating with a congressman named Richard Nixon—he may or may not have been telling the truth. Probably not, not the whole truth in any case; Chambers could never have been satisfied with being simply a foreign agent. He would have to be at least a double agent. He was quite capable of concocting a "confession" to satisfy, not merely the authorities, but some inner need to dramatize himself. Years later when he produced microfilms allegedly incriminating his sometime friend Alger Hiss, I was not surprised to learn he had kept them hidden in a pumpkin in his backyard.

Now he drew a sealed envelope from the inside pocket of his jacket and handed it to me.

"Do me a favor," he said. "Deliver this for me. You live nearby and I have to be in another part of town. I don't want to mail it."

I saw the name on the envelope was that of a man I knew to be a party functionary.

"Only be sure," Chambers added, "to give it to the man it's addressed to. Don't leave it with anybody else."

The contents might have been a love letter or a secret message or something more prosaic, it might have been anything. I did not think to ask what was in the envelope. It was not until I was following the newspaper reports on the Alger Hiss trial some years later, and the part played by Chambers in that sorry affair, that it occurred to me I would have a hard time denying I was a communist courier if he had thought to accuse me. After all, I had delivered the letter. Its contents could have been anything he said they were.

I talked to Chambers only once more, after an interval of

some years, when he surprised me with a telephone call. It was after he had become a highly paid *Time*-think ideologue and I was on the point of leaving the *Worker* to take a job with the Book-of-the-Month Club. I had wondered how so identified a communist could so readily have become a spokesman for the American anti-Soviet establishment. I should have been less naive. After all, Whittaker Chambers was not the only "known communist" who had suddenly become a known anticommunist.

Anyway the enlightened repudiator of Comrade Stalin was waiting at the other end of the line.

"Are you still down there?" he asked abruptly.

"You know how it is," I said. "Once you've had anything to do with communist . . ."

Mr. Chambers grunted, and hung up.

Recently I saw in the *New York Times* that "President Ronald Reagan announced the posthumous award of the Medal of Freedom, the government's highest civilian award, to Whittaker Chambers, the professed Soviet agent who became a celebrated anticommunist 35 years ago . . . He was cited for his contribution in the field of public service."

Chapter 30

The morning after my escape from Washington, I had hardly got to my desk when there was a phone call from the wife of the vice-president.

"You missed your profession," she said. "You should have been a television actor."

For a moment I failed to catch her drift. "You mean . . ." I was dismayed. "You mean you actually saw that thing on your TV?"

"Sure. We all did. Our leaders went to the Union Club to catch the show. Afraid the company would be named. You know . . ." She giggled. "That Red outfit in Boston . . . I guess they were disappointed not to be named. I mean you were cleared."

By the grace of Cohn and McCarthy (whose combined names reminded me of the title of an old-fashioned vaudeville act), I was forgiven. I was made whole again in the minds of my employers. In short, I was cleared.

That word "cleared" made me squirm. The sheer presumption of it. As if any citizen, or group thereof had the right to condemn politically or give political absolution to a fellow citizen whose views differed from theirs. Even more depressing was the self-righteous acceptance of the rigmarole by all those good people who had presumably been "cleared" at birth. Of such must be the kingdom of heaven.

Shortly after my return to Boston, an editor of a weekly news magazine phoned Arthur Thornhill to ask about me. "Now that Cameron's out, what are you going to do with Seaver?"

Mr. Thornhill sounded incensed. "What are you trying to do? Tell me how to run my business? Don't you know he's been cleared?"

Dry cleaned! But apparently not yet spotless. Some weeks later I had a telegram from another congressional committee headed by a senator named Jenner—if I remember correctly—a sort of poor man's McCarthy show. The message said I was to appear as a witness at the Foley Square courthouse in New York.

When I got there the committee's press representative seemed surprised. "Oh damn!" he greeted me. "I meant to tell you not to come." He pondered the somewhat embarrassing situation. "However, since you're here . . . Just a minute . . . I'll be right back."

He reappeared shortly. "Okay. The senator will see you now."

When I came into the committee room, I had a feeling my host and his fellow inquisitors had nothing to do, they were just sitting there on their hands waiting for something to happen.

As soon as I was sworn in, the wearisome litany began. "Are you now or have you ever been a member of? . . ."

After a few more standard questions put to me by the committee's black-shirted counsel, I turned to the chairman. "Look, Senator, I don't mind answering his questions, but I've already answered the same questions asked by Senator McCarthy's committee. It's all there in the record."

Mr. Jenner seemed startled, in fact somewhat flustered.

"You did?" he exclaimed. "You mean? . . ."

It occurred to me he didn't like being caught on the other gang's turf. "Oh well, in that case, as you say, there's no point."

I was about to get up from the witness chair when I was stopped by the committee's inquisitor.

"Just a minute," he commanded. "Just one minute." He was wielding aloft a much folded newspaper, perhaps in imitation of the act McCarthy had previously put on to impress gullible journalists. "I have here a copy of the Sunday edition of the *Daily Worker* in the thirties. The masthead gives the names of ten editors and yours is one of them. Now we have information that nine of these editors were known communists. Are you trying to tell us you were not a communist?"

"Never mind." The senator was waving his counsel aside. "Never mind." And turning to the witness, "We're sorry to have bothered you," he said, and even offered his hand in parting.

His fellow committee members also shook my hand, as if I were a long lost friend. It would have been comical if it was not so embarrassing.

And thus it was I left the Foley Square courthouse a twice-cleared man. Hopefully my name could now be erased from the blacklist of those suspected of "disloyalty" by—and to—the self-appointed caretakers of "loyalty."

Chapter 31

By now I had been with Little, Brown enough years to consider myself a member of the wedding. Or so I thought. Until one day I was told that when someone at a recent directors' meeting happened to mention I was a Jew, director-in-chief Arthur Thornhill exclaimed: "I never knew *that*!"

My informant was not being malicious, merely normal. Indeed he seemed to find our leader's explosion rather amusing, he being quite broad-minded about anti-Semitism and such things.

"In case you're thinking of ever becoming a director yourself," he added as an afterthought, midway between a sneer and a chuckle.

Not that Mr. Thornhill was prejudiced, as he himself had explained to me in the early days of our association when he had no idea I might belong to a suspect tribe.

He was telling me about a confession Alfred MacIntyre, his predecessor in office, had once made to him.

It seemed that he and Mr. MacIntyre were busy playing golf one day when who did they see approaching them but Bennett Cerf, a fellow publisher, head of Random House.

"I was so embarrassed," Mr. MacIntyre confessed later to

Mr. Thornhill. "Because you know I like Bennett. But he's a Jew and our club doesn't admit Jews."

"And I said to him," Mr. Thornhill said to me, "Alfred you're a snob."

Which at least suggested a new name for anti-Semitism.

Although I had been living in liberal New England ever since my sixteenth year, I was slow to learn the mores of the Yankees. I was into my second decade with Little, Brown before the treasurer leaked a secret he had apparently kept on ice—or should I say, on his mind—all that time.

"Those flowers," he confided, those flowers I had found in my recently rented Pinckney Street rooms on returning home from my first day on the job . . . those flowers . . . Had I supposed they were some kind of welcome gift from the firm (as I had in fact naively thought they might be). Nothing of the sort. They had actually been ordered by a *secretary* who had the *audacity* to charge them to the company.

I remember another colleague telling me that a well-to-do bachelor uncle of his had died without leaving a cent for the family. "And do you know what we found out?" he said. "The sonofabitch had been living on his capital."

His indignation reminded me of the Boston lady who, being told that a woman they both knew was so hard up she had actually resorted to prostitution, declared: "How perfectly dreadful! Before I did that I would dip into my capital."

There will always be a Boston, I thought as I listened to the treasurer's tale of the incredible secretary.

This way to the egress!

"You're quitting just when you're getting to be useful to us." Mr. Thornhill flattered me when I ventured to suggest it was time for me to resign.

To paraphrase a homily I believe was voiced by the then

recently elected president of our country: Ask not what has the company done for you. Ask rather what have you done for the company.

Some ten years later when I was working in New York as editor of a small publishing house, the realization dawned on me I was not supposed to go on forever.

I was in my eighty-second year. It was time to get off the treadmill.

Chapter 32

Seeking to conclude this random chronicle, I am like the man who was condemned to be hanged but was granted one last wish before he was put to death. His wish was that he might choose the tree for his hanging. Alas! He could not find the right tree in the whole forest.

"If I had more time," he sighed when his fate ultimately ran out of patience and there could be no further delay.

"If . . ." The little word that encompasses so much.

If "I" . . . The even littler word.

If I had more time.

"Time," my dictionary says, is "the succession of states of the universe regarded as a whole in which any state is either before or after every other."

Which explains everything.

But why not say simply, without fol-de-rol: "Time is"?

As simply as we say, or might say if we could ever rid ourselves of the urge to explain the inexplicable: "I am."

Time is the element in which I move and have my being,

as ineluctably as a fish lives in water. For me, as for every living thing, only death is outside of time.

Which is where I fancy I was for some hours after I suffered a stroke. Not so bad a state to be in, I thought as I lay in bed in the hospital where an ambulance had brought me the night before, a breathing corpse.

"You were lucky," said the doctor when he visited my bed the following day. There would come a time, he promised, when I might have another stroke. That one could be more serious, if indeed it did not finish me altogether.

"How do you feel?" he asked before departing, by way of consolation.

"Perishable," I thought.

One moment you're at home having a leisurely after-dinner conversation with whomever, when suddenly, unaccountably, your tongue has become heavy in your mouth . . . sluggish words . . . clog . . . your . . . And the next moment you wake up in a hospital.

"But darling," my wife says soothingly as if to an ailing child, "it wasn't a moment. It took hours. They had a whole crew working on you.

"You mean I'm still me? How did *you* get here?"

"Same way as you. Same time. Same ambulance. They didn't want to let me go with you but I insisted. You were pretty sick and I was pretty frightened?"

And I was pretty fortunate to have such a loving comrade, I was thinking when another doctor appeared. This one was in plain clothes. Uninvited he drew up a chair and seated himself by my bed.

"Now," he said, "tell me everything."

I saw my wife slap her hand to her mouth to stifle a laugh, but all I could manage was an astonished grin.

Now tell me everything!

As if one could!

As if one had actually experienced what happened when!

Mulling over the incident later I thought my inquisitive visitor might only have been the staff psychiatrist giving me a quick "brain scan" to see if I still had all my marbles.

It's a question I have often asked myself.

"In old age," as Samuel Butler mused in *The Way of All Flesh,* "we live under the shadow of death, which, like the sword of Damocles, may descend at any moment, but we have so long found life to be an affair of being rather frightened than hurt we have become like the people who live under Vesuvius and chance it without much misgiving."

Also, Butler could have added, without much awareness they were chancing anything unusual. Like most of us do—or rather don't—most of our days. Whether we are living under Vesuvius or merely crossing the street.

According to story, Damocles was a member of the court of Dionysius the Elder, tyrant of Syracuse, who ordered him to sit at a banquet under a sword suspended by a single hair. "To demonstrate the precariousness of a king's fortune" my dictionary explains.

I wonder about Damocles.

Was he the nervous type? Did he suffer from indigestion? Did he question the tyrant's way of demonstrating a king's worries? Like, why isn't the sword hanging over his head instead of mine?

"By my rambling digressions I perceive myself to be grown old." The words are Franklin's, but I perceive the same thing about my own digressions.

Only they may not be as rambling as I like to think.

Maybe I ramble on purpose.

To hide from myself.

To delay having to face the faceless.

To escape from the vanity of despair.

The tyrant of Syracuse had only one Damocles to illustrate what was on his royal mind. But Pentagon, the American tyrant, has a far mightier sword hanging over all of us to demonstrate the precariousness of our nuclear fortunes. To emphasize which the Department of Defense spends not merely millions of the people's money, but billions, hundreds of billions. (Presently an annual "investment" of nearly three hundred billions!)

And this, mind you, when our nuclear larder is already bursting with enough deadly viands to murder all of us at the drop of a missile.

To meet, as we mindlessly assert, the "communist threat."

While our nomination for the office of "enemy" is likewise feverishly preparing to meet the "capitalist threat."

If this be sanity which way to the madhouse?

Talk about chancing it!

How many Vesuviuses are necessary for us to realize the danger of our being hurt rather than frightened (to twist Samuel Butler's meaning)?

Consider the fate of the gentleman from Hiroshima. Presumably he was only waiting for the bank to open that August morning over forty years ago. Meanwhile he must have been sitting on one of the lower steps leading up to the bank.

After the holocaust the clocks agreed. It was just ten minutes after eight in the morning.

This was the moment time stopped. The moment the first nuclear bomb announced the birth of a new age—if any.

What had all this to do with the gentleman from Hiroshima. He had disappeared in a flash! He had been reduced in a split second to a mere shadow of himself. Only his shade remained waiting for the bank to open.

But the bank, too, had disappeared in the same flash.